MW01672093

COSMIC INTELLIGENCE

SYNC IN WITH THE CREATION

COSMIC INTELLIGENCE

SYNC IN WITH THE CREATION

SHISHIRENDU KUMAR JHA

Copyright © 2022 Shishirendu Kumar Jha

Paperback: 978-1-63767-636-3
Hardcover: 978-1-63767-735-3
eBook: 978-1-63767-637-0
Library of Congress Control Number: 2021923876

All rights reserved. No part of this publication may be reproduced, distributed, or transmitted in any form or by any electronic or mechanical means, without the prior written permission of the publisher, except in the case of brief quotations embodied in critical reviews and certain other noncommercial uses permitted by copyright law.

Ordering Information:

BookTrail Agency
8838 Sleepy Hollow Rd.
Kansas City, MO 64114

Printed in the United States of America

This is the path to truth.
May people need your message

– Ajahn Brahamali
(Bodhiyana Monastery, Perth, Australia)

DEDICATION

पिता स्वर्गः पिता धर्मः पिता हि परमंतपः ।

पितरोप्रीतमापन्ने प्रियन्ते सर्व देवताः ।।

Father is heaven, father is dharma, he is the ultimate presence of my life. If he is happy, God is happy.

– Mahabharat

नास्ति मातृसमच्छाया नास्ति मातृसमं गतिः।

नास्ति मातृसमं त्राणः नास्ति मातृसमं प्रपा ।।

There is no shade like mother. There is no resort like mother, there is no security like mother, no other ever giving fountain of life.

– Skanad Purana

CONTENTS

Dedication vii
Acknowledgment xiii
About the Author xv
Preface xvii
Foreword xix

Chapter 1: Introduction 1
Nothing Is in Human Control 1
Cosmic Intelligence Can Connect Us with Higher Energy Which Controls Us 6
Formation of the Universe Until Evolution 9
Worrying about Uncontrollable is Useless. . . . 12
Idea Humans Have of Identity and Existence. 14
Our Existence Follows the Pattern of the Universe 16

Chapter 2: The Existence 18
Our Existence Is Dependent on Living and Non-Living Beings Around Us 18
My Eternal Self Is Always Watching My Transient Self 22
Focusing On the True Nature of "I" 25

Other People's Influences Form a Person's Existence.......... 29
Existence Has Multiple Parts 31
Happiness Is Misunderstood 33

Chapter 3: The Body and the Action.......... 36
Body and Mind, Separate or Inseparable?.... 36
Body and The Action.......... 41
Three Qualities of Nature 43
Sattva and Cosmic Intelligence.......... 46
Types of Actions in Three Gunas.......... 47
Cosmos Provides the Intelligence.......... 51

Chapter 4: The Body 54
Destruction and Formation - Nature of the Cosmos 54
The Ultimate Bliss.......... 61
Elements of Nature 64

Chapter 5: The Element.......... 68
Essential Elements of Life.......... 68
Five Fundamental Factors of Existence...... 71
The Five Senses 78

Chapter 6: The Mind.......... 81
Formation of the Mind.......... 87
Parts of the Mind.......... 91
Nature of the Mind 96
The No Mind Situation 96

Chapter 7: The Energy Realm 100
Chakras 101
Root Chakra 105
Sacral Chakra. 107
Solar Chakra 108
Heart Chakra. 109
Throat Chakra 111
Third Eye Chakra 112
Crown Chakra 113

Chapter 8: The Moment. 115
No Mind and The Dilemma of Being Present 116
Involve in Everything but Entangle in Nothing 119
Think in Broader Terms. 121
You are the Cosmic Intelligence 122
Experience the Moment 123

Chapter 9: Accessing the Cosmos 127
Significance of Meditation for Me 127
Meditation 129
My Experience with Meditation 133
The Tap Water Dilemma 134
The Anahat Naad 137
Beyond the Anahat. 140
Fly High 141
Circular Geometrical Object 144
The Blue Sun 144

Chapter 10: Practise and Exercise to Activate the Cosmic Intelligence . . 147
Accessing Cosmic Intelligence 151
Cosmic Energy and Meditation 155
My next releases 163

ACKNOWLEDGMENT

This book is the result of motivation from a lot of people. It is because of my elder brother, Shardindu, that I could start writing this book. His motivation, continuous support, and encouragement resulted in the current form of this book. My younger brother, Purnendu provided me with input on various Yoga techniques. He has been a guide to the people suffering from various lifestyle diseases, some of which are referenced in this book. My youngest brother, Bimlendu, was helpful in keeping my website in sync with this book and, most importantly, my wife Khushi and kids Shree, Shuv, and Shambhavi were great motivators while facing difficult times.

Apart from them I express my sincere gratitude to my Guru, "Sadhguru" and various other people who are contributing towards the consciousness of the whole planet by their books, podcasts, speeches, and other means. To name a few: Dr. Deepak Chopra, Alexender Fairman, Ekart Tole, Dr. Joe Dispenza, Mark Wolyn, Sri Sri Ravi Shankar, etc.

ABOUT THE AUTHOR

Shishirendu Kumar Jha

A yogi by nature, a devotee by tradition, a hermit by attitude, a Statistician by education, and last but not least a healer by instinct. A crusader for healing the physical and mental sufferings of mankind. Equipped with the treasure of traditional, spiritual, and occult knowledge, path-breaking techniques, and scientific examination of problems. He is a unique combination of conventional methods and unconventional techniques to answer the problems of suffering humanity.

A natural healer, an expert in diverse techniques like hypnotherapy, sound healing, healing based on family constellation, dream therapy, an expert in lucid dreaming, Chakra analyzing, energy scanning to put an end to big and small problems of life. Capable of recognizing emotional and metaphysical reasons behind the problems and prescribing simple solutions about lifestyle, food habits, dreaming patterns, and mirror imaging. He can stimulate your subconscious mind to extract information and plant thought for a permanent solution. An impeccable track record of healing fears and phobias. Has guided innumerable people in getting rid of evil habits and inculcating great hobbies. A world spiritual leader in self-hypnosis, meditation, and breathing techniques taking humanity closure to bliss is the goal.

PREFACE

Who do you think you are? A physical body of flesh and bones or a spiritual consciousness? I believe your answer would be both, right? But is that really the truth?

When was the last time you actively developed a conscious thought? Can't remember? Don't worry, it happens to the best of us. Most of us stop actively producing thoughts once we get out of our comfy showers and step out into the day-to-day hustle and bustle of life, where, ironically, we need those thoughts the most.

Due to this, most of us live out our lives on autopilot without ever noticing the lack of conscious thoughts and actions. However, it doesn't have to be that way. This active and conscious side of us doesn't go anywhere; it still resides in there somewhere, silently watching all our actions. Here, in this book we not only venture through the physical and emotional but dive even deeper inside a life to decipher the most minuscule of predicaments an individual face. It's only a matter of activating this side of us that is aware, conscious, and intelligent; which leads us to the basis of this book; Cosmic Intelligence.

Cosmic Intelligence refers to the ability to mass synchronize and orchestrate every living cell in your body and bring order to your 'self' amidst the chaotic day to day commotion of life. In this book, you will learn how to achieve cosmic intelligence and use it to better your life. You will learn about the part of you that is silent, a system inside that is better than the default one, an intelligence that is infinite and cosmic.

So, if you think, you know who you are…think again.

FOREWORD

(Swami Yogeshwaranand)

The entire concept of Cosmic Intelligence has been elucidated by the author in a manner par excellence. The greatest success of the author lies in his effort to link Cosmic Intelligence to human existence for healing all kind of mental and physical pain.

I congratulate the author for propounding this novel philosophical concept to serve humanity. The author has presented the rare combination of unparalleled scholarship with deep spiritual realization. This book is an excellent product of his technological skill to analyze and disciplined way to carve out the boundaries of this revolutionary philosophical concept called "Cosmic Intelligence". Vedanta also propounds the same omnipotent and all-pervading force which is one but appears to be many because of Maya. While the whole world is marred by the parochial and aggressive indoctrination the choice of name is most secular and free from all bias.

The comprehension with the object and action can't be just intellectual but it is experiential. He is successful in comparing three Gunas of the cosmos called, Satva,

Rajas and Tamas. The moment thought is separated from the action and it is free from all identities, the path of liberation is attained. His perspicuous endeavor in establishing various entry points such as body, mind and energy to go inward is quite commendable.

This book is not only for them who are seeking spiritual success, but this is also for them who want solace from the stressful daily work schedule OR what not.

CHAPTER 1
INTRODUCTION

"You Are the Universe Experiencing Itself."
– Alan Watts

Nothing Is in Human Control

Humans have thought of ourselves as a pretty big deal for millennia. Then along came science, and it taught us how insignificant we are. Or maybe, not that insignificant, and the universe only becomes real because we are looking at it. We were created in this universe without our will, and it also destroys us against our will. We are all natural because we cannot control the things within ourselves or around us. The thoughts in our minds and the emotions rising in our hearts, never took our permission to evolve. Our blood has been given free will to fill in our veins neither does our heart need permission to beat nor our kidneys to filter the blood.

My mind runs through these thoughts, and this has not been habitual, but after my transformation into a conscious human being. So before moving forward into the deep beliefs I have been holding to share with the readers, I consider it necessary for my readers to know me well. This might help them sort out the experiences I have lived through their interpretation.

It was never easy to be second among four brothers. My elder brother was extraordinarily brilliant and outstanding in all sorts of activities. The brother younger than me was weak as a child. Due to his illness, he got most of the extra needed attention from my parents. So, it was natural for the youngest brother to get all the attention; he was also the youngest in the family.

Since childhood, I was a timid boy who could get into a difficult situation too quickly and couldn't speak up about my side of the story. I was an average student who would work hard to get good grades. But, even if things were nice and going well, still somewhere deep down in my heart, I felt life was not fair to me and kept blaming everyone around me.

Slowly, I found myself surrounded by so many mental issues, such as not being good enough, not being happy; otherwise, things would go wrong, keeping silent to avoid confrontation, always keeping a low profile so that people would not notice me, and many more. I made a virtual wall around myself, where I kept my vulnerable side. When you feel weak, subconsciously, you try to be strong and need to compensate for it by some of your bad habits. That's how I started eating recklessly and became 125 kg. Soon, I developed high blood pressure and became pre-diabetic; I had migraines since I was in class 9th, and I had stomach issues, counting a few. I used to be under great stress and was angry with everything present and happening around me most of the time. Unnecessarily, I became too egoistic to handle. I kept switching my jobs because I didn't like the bosses, and sometimes I left due to a desire to earn more, which kept me unstable throughout my career.

My family and relationships were tottering. I stopped talking to everyone around me. I thought people hurt me intentionally. The smallest of things made me feel for hours. Slowly, I developed the condition of depression. In 2015, I made the biggest mistake of my life that changed me forever. I had a very bad fight with my father. Before that, I tried never to hurt my parents in any situation. But a series of incidents took place or, better to say, my mind made me see what I wanted to see. On the occasion of my cousin's marriage, when many guests were present at my home, I thought I would have to clear this in front of everyone. Perhaps destiny was taking me towards my goal through an undesirable path. Your near and dear ones play a significant role in your transformation, and I was no exception.

After a few days, I realised that it was not me and started digging into myself. I found that I was full of psychological issues. I thought to go to a Hypnotherapist to clear them out, but later, I thought it would be good to learn this. Hence, I became certified in Hypnotherapy.

Similarly, I explored other healing modalities such as sound healing, crystal healing, shaman, family constellation, relaxation techniques, Reiki, and Lama-Fera techniques. All these modalities talk about making your belief system stronger. But none teaches how. I realised that they all are superficial techniques. If you are lucky, they will work and resolve your issue. My elder brother spent a significant amount of time in the lower Himalayas, meditating; he suggested that I meditate. He also showed me the 8-fold system of meditation. I started meditating. Initially, it wasn't easy to sit even for five minutes. Later, my guru (Sadhguru) from South India showed me how to deal with those disturbing thoughts. Gradually, I increased it to two hours every day. The journey from five minutes to two hours was enlightening. I had few experiences in the way. I started seeing my thoughts clearly and observed changing my emotions. I understood the actual meaning of 'I.' A time came when I could stop all my thoughts. I could control my food. Now I couldn't become agitated so quickly in an argument. I stopped wanting to win an argument all the time. I found that my body has become calm, and my mind is calmer. After practising it for 10-12 months, all the physical issues started to vanish.

I stopped taking pills for my hypertension. The prediabetic condition was reversed. I did get a headache, but it was not so intense. Even colds and coughs were not as frequent as they used to be.

And the time came when I realised how small we are. In this vast universe, we keep our self-esteem so big that our intelligence, memory, and intellect start creating a problem for us. As long as my thoughts and emotions were driving me, I had always been piqued. When I started driving my emotions, life became easier, restful, and serene. I realised when I observe my thoughts that I am not biased with my emotions. I realised it had been present earlier, but back then, my thoughts were more powerful and feelings so persuasive that I had to obey them. Now "Cosmic Intelligence" enabled me to know what thoughts are worth following and which emotions are good to feel. It also provides more energy, willpower, and continuous perseverance to fight my bad side. Life has changed completely. I activated the intelligence provided by the cosmos in me.

Today, when I want to share my life experience with people, I also want to share the techniques with you. I know every person has this right to know about one's eternal self.

The point is, it all happened as it was written to happen. It was not me controlling the situation, nor my guru who dedicated his time to teaching me. We cannot control a single moment in our lives or even a single function of our body. A more robust mechanism works outside our consciousness that has sent us into this world among a distinct set of people. This mechanism constantly creates situations that help us develop our personalities.

One such example that we are being taken care of by a higher energy source is presented by animals eating, reproducing, and living in their habitats. A cub is taken care of by its parents from any kind of harm. The lioness fights tooth and claw to defend their cubs. Squabs are kept in a secure shelter by their parents. Since it cannot fly, the mother pigeon feeds it by bringing food into the nest. These are the laws of nature, and each creature is aligned with them. Similar is our existence; our survival depends on a higher energy source that protects us. We are identical to those vulnerable baby animals that need protection. The system is already there for us and making us adopt habits that facilitate our survival. Our memory, intellect, and emotions evolve as we grow old, and we understand that the world is not a safer place. In the majority of the cases, we become apprehensive about our life events that never occur. Our intellect and experiences make us understand the realities of life.

Cosmic Intelligence Can Connect Us with Higher Energy Which Controls Us

Not all, but many of us believe in the higher energy source that has created our beings to make them survive the situations we live in. Focusing on these thoughts, nature, the productivity and forcing them to depths solely depend on our capabilities. In the broader plane, that higher energy source is controlling us. It surrounds us with situations that lead to our development at different levels, eventually harnessing our distinct personality traits. Unfortunately, most of us spend our time on this planet thinking with an illusion that our life belongs to us. With the limited free will we are granted, we claim to live life on our terms. This is precisely against the fundamentals of existence, and these perspectives take us away from the very nature of our reality.

You might be confused about how our free will is limited when free? It sounds more like an oxymoron—Limited Free Will. To understand this, I will give an example from my childhood. I still remember, I used to accompany my uncle while he was taking the cattle to graze the grass. He used to tie the cattle in the middle of the pasture and sit away from them and watch them from a certain distance. The cow could graze the grass anywhere within the area of the circle defined by the length of the rope as radius but couldn't eat the grass outside the area of the circle. The whole territory within the circle was cow's free will to carry, but she was not allowed to control the mechanisms outside that circle. That's how our free will works. Although we can control some aspects, the higher source contains all of us beyond the boundaries of our imagination. Or maybe we can say that the higher source is taking care of us by moulding our decisions and behaviour for our good. We need that source for our survival. Our body is hardware, and the mind is the software. To keep them working, they need a source of higher energy. This has been termed as energy realm. Science has now proved that energy cannot be destroyed, energy transfer is real in waves, and the vibrations are what it takes for the waves to move. All objects within the universe are vibrating. This is the essential nature of the source. We cannot be different from our source.

So, what should be our purpose in this universe? The broadly grasped idea is to align ourselves with the universe. Whatever we experience is essentially conducted through the spine, as the neurons travel across the spine to deliver a message to the brain. There will be no experience if the spine is dislocated. Since the spine is basing the context of our experience, it has been regarded as the axis of the universe. With research, we have come to know that the whole solar system is the small blob in the cosmos. Our experience makes us go after certain things and avoid others. Understanding this division of consciousness makes the knowledge of ultimate unity challenging to understand. Your spine first experiences everything you sense, see, hear, and touch. You will understand your experiences and realities beforehand if you master the consciousness. The energy chakras are also situated in the spine. Chakra means energy points in your body. These chakras are thought to be the spinning disks of energy that must stay open and aligned as they correspond to a bundle of nerves, major organs, and areas of our energetic body that affect our emotional and physical well-being. These chakras will be explained further in a separate chapter to be comprehended in more detail.

It is not the complexity of the external situation that is doing this, and it is just that we are not determining the nature of our experience within ourselves. Once we understand this level of consciousness, we can activate cosmic intelligence and understand the realities of life and the universe based on the context of our experience.

That is the place where you identify the presence of a higher energy source controlling you all. It's not visible; it cannot be heard, touched but felt with intuition, sixth sense, meditation, the gut feeling, and higher consciousness. The journey is never easy, but once you get to know the revelations within, you can better feel the existence of a higher energy source. You think it's a need for your very existence. Our reality is dependent on this source. With the insurmountable complexities of life, we cannot deal with every situation ourselves unless we have faith that we will make out of it. It's all in our heads and hearts that makes us unique from other known creatures on this planet. The wisdom, thought process, conscious mind, distinct feelings, emotions, empathy, compassion, intellect, and whatnot. It's not your fault that you became the victim of psychological issues, nor was your intention to develop your personality this way. It was your surrounding that tangled your mental health in such matters. It was your unique surviving and coping strategies that made you the human you have become. Eventually, it's the higher source that unknowingly helps us, making us resilient and competitive enough, making us harness the personality traits that we specifically need to live life.

Formation of the Universe Until Evolution

Cosmic intelligence refers to the generation, synchronisation, and orchestration of many complex chemical reactions inside every one of our trillions of body cells. In simple terms, the universe is chaos without order because it will directly lead to destruction. But the chaos in order is cosmic intelligence. For example, if a single thing like water, temperature, fire, or air is missing, it will not be easy for us to survive. The chaos has some order because the entire universe has its intelligence, harnessing energy and power. The cosmos around us is harnessing power, and energy. Therefore, it has its intelligence. It responds to your prayers, thoughts, and being because it is intelligent. For now, you are sitting inside living energy. To understand the depths of cosmic intelligence, it would be necessary to peek into the universe's formation from a theoretical perspective.

The universe is a powerful mechanism, controlled by something even more critical, with innumerable galaxies, planets, and stars complementing each other. But if we talk about the total space, it takes just 0.00-001%. The making of the universe follows an event of destruction. One widely accepted Big Bang Theory of science claims that the universe's formation started by the collapse of a high-density particle with massive energy called a big bang. The universe's construction began roughly 13.8 billion years ago, and it is thus considered the age of the universe. It took 10^{-43} seconds to give birth to space and time; in another 10^{-6} seconds, it took the shape of the universe after the Big Bang[1]. After three seconds of the Big Bang, a positively charged mass called proton and a neutral mass called neutron developed in the nucleus for the essential elements like Helium and Hydrogen. After 300 million years of forming the nucleus, stars and galaxies took birth from the cosmic specs. Even our solar system took its form five billion years ago. It all started as it was meant to create the universe and everything in it, taking its directions from the real source. These phenomena were not directed by me or anyone; they happened without our willingness or even our knowledge, but we are linked.

---

1 Williams, Matt., (2015). What is the Big Bang Theory? https://phys.org/news/2015-12-big-theory.html

> *"The nitrogen in our DNA, the calcium in our teeth, the iron in our blood, the carbon in our apple pies were made in the interiors of collapsing stars. We are made of star-stuff."*
>
> – Carl Sagan, Cosmos

Based on the Big Bang Theory, before forming the universe, all matter was compacted into a tiny ball with intense heat and infinite density called a Singularity. As the universe was created and expanded, the essential nature of creation remained the same. Formation of a nucleus surrounded by revolving electrons forming the atoms and the formation of stars, planets, and galaxy system, all bound by the force that keeps them intact. No planet or star or even a speck of dust was left behind to function independently. During the Big Bang explosion, every atom was provided sufficient force and support to join, collide, and merge to form the more significant objects of the universe. Without the considerable destruction, this construction would not have any meaning. Every particle was equipped with intelligence to evolve through its final state. This destruction was meant for the reason of creation of others. An asteroid entering the orbit may or may not hit the planet as no one, but the universe itself guides it. One such collision wiped all the Dinosaurs from Earth 65 million years ago and brought about the creation of man. Cosmically intelligent phenomena happen for reasons; the destruction of one star creates many other satellites, meteorites, and planets. That's how cosmic intelligence works for the universe, and eventually, for us.

> *"We have a genetic kinship with all life on earth, an atomic kinship to all matter in the cosmos. So, when I look at the universe, I feel large because I remind myself that not only are we living in this universe, the universe is living within us."*
>
> – Neil deGrasse Tyson

Worrying about Uncontrollable is Useless

As human beings, many times we regret things we can't control in life. It's natural; it's something not to worry about. This worrying is the reflective reaction of our hopelessness when we encounter unexpected and undesired experiences. No matter how hard we try to control, we are not made so. We can't control the disease we might get in the future, we can't control ageing, we can't control death, and we can't control loss. We all are struggling just because we have an illusion that we can control certain aspects of life. If we understand that we are not given this authority to control things, it might be peaceful for us to accept the realities of life. The way the human mind is designed, the most challenging aspect it encounters is acceptance after long-term denial. If we accept the truth, we might help others struggling with the same situation. We are made from nature, so every emotion and feeling we encounter is natural and not man-made. A grievance after loss, happiness after buying a car, stress before an exam; these natural aspects are part of our nature that can't be controlled—just accepting nature as it brings much contentment in life compared to things brought by denial.

Activating cosmic intelligence will make our thoughts positive and help us deal with emotions. This tool will help in life crises (emotional, physical, financial, etc.) Cosmic intelligence can not only help us embrace unique skills but can also help us in dealing with the challenges of life. We can deal with the emotional crisis by understanding the movements of stars and their implications on us and planet Earth. We can understand the physical effects by embracing cosmic intelligence, such as understanding the impact of the law of the universe on our beings, health, traits, relationships, and habits. We can understand and deal with the financial crisis by foreseeing them through unique intuitive skills of cosmic intelligence. The more you become receptive and open to cosmic intelligence and embrace it, you will move towards Cosmic Insight, Divine Revelations, Higher Wisdom, Wholeness Experiences, Supernatural Intuition, Absolute Truth and Justice, and Selfless Love. And above all, our ability to keep our inner self-calm in any sort of turmoil. The law of consciousness theorises that the outer world reflects of the inner world. Our inner world always communicates with us. For the most part, though, we ignore it. When your inner world is in disarray, the best thing you can do is stop and figure out what is happening inside. This can help you reduce the chaos in your outer world. It appears that if we can harness the abilities of cosmic intelligence, we can harness abilities to calm our inner and outer worlds, and we might be better able to understand the realities of life and act accordingly.

Idea Humans Have of Identity and Existence

Human beings are entangled with their earthly objects such as education, job, family, society, and relationships. So much so that they think they are making a balance between so many different attributes of life. In this effort, we subconsciously ignore various aspects of our existence. When asked about their identity, people start talking about their name, father's name, the place they belong to, or the work they do for a living. But none of them seems correct. Others give a name; of course, people adopt new names and like to be called by that name. Hence, the name can't be one's real identity. We can't be identified by our father's or forefather's identity. When a person says he belongs to a particular city/street/place, he has mistaken the location with his identity. Neither does his job reflect ultimately who he is. All different attributes which a person thinks they are identified by are wrong. Therefore, a person's identity is a complex enigma that his consciousness and learning must reveal. Their job, background, ancestral tree, culture, and language do not define the identity but rather a mere reflection of where they have adopted to live and what coping mechanisms they have adopted to survive. Then the question arises, who are we? Who is experiencing good, bad, and ugly incidents of life? Who is working hard to meet both ends, who lives in the city/village/street? The answer is straightforward and very complex. The concept of human identity has been linked to the idea of existence. Our existence is not an isolated life. It is dependent on the other living and non-living beings around us. The cosmos has provided a conducive environment to flourish. An optimum distance from the sun for the creation to survive, an exact mixture of the gases to keep us breathing, a precise amount of water to sustain life, all the flora and fauna to support life. The list is never-ending.

Our existence is not dependent only on this body. Several factors are part of our existence. Any imbalance in those factors creates lots of problems with our existence. For example, we see our surroundings and find that everyone is suffering. Some people suffer because they don't have enough money to feed their children; some are not happy as their children are away and don't bother if they are alive or dead; there are people with relationship problems, health problems, etc. It all happens because of the imbalance of those vital factors. Five of these essential factors are space, air (intellectual), water (emotional), fire (spiritual), and earth (practical). Our existence is dependent on the presence of these universal factors, and alignment with the patterns of the universe allows us to fulfil the purpose of our existence. Existence is not possible if we take out any one of these five essential elements. Each element is associated with one more sense.

Our Existence Follows the Pattern of the Universe

Our existence, by default, follows the patterns of the universe in a way a drama follows the script written for it. The designs of the universe are identified and recurred in different contexts, sometimes even modelled mathematically. Natural patterns of the universe include spirals, trees, waves, symmetries, meanders, tessellations, stripes, and foams. Early Greek philosophers studied the patterns of the universe, where Pythagoras, Plato, and Empedocles attempted to explain the order in nature. But it doesn't mean that our existence follows these mathematical patterns, as they are incomprehensible for many.

A small glimpse of the universe's cyclic pattern can be found in the change of seasons, changing day and night. The pattern is found in the human by way of inhaling and exhaling, contraction, and expansion. A woman's body follows the cycle of the moon and so on. We have heard from our elders that discipline is a must in one's life. People without discipline always suffer in their life. It is essential to follow the pattern of the universe. They are vital for our existence. Some patterns of our physical body are similar to those of the universe. For example, the Earth has 72% water; the same is true for our physical bodies. Our body comprises 72% water. With a slight shift in the cosmos, like the moon coming closer to the earth in the whole moon night, the water level rises in the ocean. It happens with the human body as well. A person with strong emotions shows different emotional patterns on the full moon day.

All the five essential elements are necessary for our physical body to sustain life. Life has been made by the cosmos so that each component is required for the existence of our life. As water constitutes 72% of our body, the air is a must for breathing and keeping us alive.

All these revelations direct us towards the fact that we are all connected with the universe somehow but unable to comprehend the divinity behind it. Our existence is dependent on the universe and the things created within. Without these universal elements, our survival would not have been possible. 'Survival of the fittest' highlights not only the fittest beings surviving on Earth but also the intelligent, conscious beings who use their intellect for growth, prosperity, and legacy for the next generations to live in a better way.

CHAPTER 2
THE EXISTENCE

Our Existence Is Dependent on Living and Non-Living Beings Around Us

Do you ever feel you are being watched all the time? If your answer is 'YES,' do you still ignore the stalker and keep doing your work. Are you aware of this stalker? Are you afraid of this person? Whether you agree, we all are being watched by ourselves all the time. Sometimes, we keep away from doing something terrible; sometimes, we don't care and do what we need. Our senses give us this capability to experience the outside world, but how can we experience our inner-self, and if it can be experienced, what is to be experienced?

> *"Every living thing is both a whole system in and of itself as well as an essential part of other systems."*
>
> – Meredith L. Young-Sowers

Suppose we are sitting in our room and watching TV. We can watch TV and understand the content. The TV and I are two different objects. I am watching the TV, and TV is being watched by me. In the same way, if I can watch my thought, then I can be a watcher, and my thought is watched. It is true for all senses. "I" is always watching me when I am awake, when I go to the office, when I am filing my taxes, when I am watching TV, when I am sneaking on someone, I am making mistakes deliberately when I am cunning with someone. All the good and bad parts of me are being observed by me all the time.

> *Water is the mirror that can show us what we cannot see. It is the blueprint for our reality, which can change with a single, positive thought. All it takes is faith if you're open to it*
>
> – Masaru Emoto

As we hold an insurmountable consciousness in our physically existing being, the same is the case with each element of the universe. A simple example is water, made of two atoms of hydrogen and one atom of oxygen. Water in the liquid state is widely available, followed by solid and gaseous states. We don't bother about how many electrons, protons, or neutrons each atom of hydrogen or oxygen have. A person who does not have any background in chemistry may not know about the chemical bonding of water and its existence in three forms. Going one step ahead, a great scientist, Masuro

Emoto, had done a tremendous amount of work on the consciousness of the water molecule. In his studies, he proved that a water molecule changes its molecular shape when exposed to different emotions. They all are other aspects of water, which we hardly bother to find out. Hence the current status of any object is only dependent on our experience with the thing. But in reality, the existence of that object is by far more significant than its current status.

Our experiences lead us to make interpretations out of scenarios in life. For example, different people hold different opinions about one person because they all had different experiences with this person. I remember my experiences with my father when I was a child. Because of his strict attitude with my elder brother, I had different opinions about him. My elder brother frequently complained about this. I was quite shy and reserved and was annoyed by others intruding in my space.

Similarly, I also avoided intruding on someone else's space as much as possible. On the other hand, my elder brother is very outgoing and authoritative. He led all the cousins and kids of our age in the village in all mischief we did. It happened so many times that even though we all are partners in his crime, he was being caught all the time and questioned and punished. Finally, after so many years, my brother asked my dad why he had always been unfair. My father gave him a simple reply; I still remember that: "You were eldest among all, so if you behave well, your younger brother/sisters will also behave well. Hence, sometimes I had to be a bit strict with you." I am not sure if that was good parenting or bad parenting then, but when I became a parent, I made sure that I would not hold my elder son responsible for what my younger son did or vice-versa. Hence opinion is created based on our experience. But the question is, how can you make your opinion right about someone, or in other words, how can the current state of someone be identified correctly? It is possible only when we see the broad picture. So, our state plays a significant role in defining others' (experiencing them) current state.

We rely on the living and non-living beings around us. Among those non-living are food, shelter, clothing, machines used for routine activities, air, water, fire, and several other inanimate objects. The living beings we rely on include plants, animals, microorganisms, and the people around us. This reliance is natural as we are made to need all these living and non-living elements in our lives. Living things need non-living things to survive. Without food, air, and water, living things die. Just like us, plants also rely on other non-living elements. They use carbon dioxide from perspective, water from the soil, and energy from sunlight to make their food. This intertwining between living and non-living things reflects their dependence on each other and indicates their essentiality. Despite knowing what we need to live and survive, we are far from recognising what is required to know our true selves. We are tricked into identifying our beings as this body-mind, which is only a costume we are given to pass through life stages.

My Eternal Self Is Always Watching My Transient Self

Eternal self refers to a person's real self, beyond ego or false self. It is often referred to as soul or spirit and indicates our true self or the essence that underlies our existence. On the contrary, the transient self is temporary, exhibiting the factors of this transient physical body that helps us live and survive on earth. It is necessary to distinguish between them to find the "I" within me. With all the worldly hustle, "I" within me has become so insignificant that we don't bother to take its opinion. We are far from recognising the true nature of "I." There is an error in identification. We identify ourselves by this body and mind.

> *"No one is born nor does anyone die; everything is eternal."*
>
> – Shiva Negi

The body and mind are the products of this environment in which we are born and brought up. Our perception of identifying ourselves can't go beyond these two parts: the body and mind. There stands the question of our existence. Do we exist as a physical body, or is it just our mind tricked into seeing as physical beings eating, drinking, sleeping, reproducing, and living to survive? Do we exist, or are we mere reflections of what has already happened? Your consciousness is your sole source to the answers. Our physical being depends on the surroundings, the living and non-living being in the environment. We cannot deny the fact that we depend on the universe and its elements for our survival. We contemplate our lifestyle, worldly desires, standards, and morals, yet we fail to look for theQ needs of our inner self. Consider how unhappy some people are who have everything of the external worlds to satisfy their desire and how happy some people are who have nothing but the satisfaction of their inner self. Many famous people have lived miserable lives and committed suicide despite having great friends, money, love, success, attention, or any external condition one can imagine. Yet, they were agitated, unsatisfied, unhappy, and lacked the realisation of what their inner self needed.

On the contrary, other people are happy despite being unable to see or walk, live in poverty, live alone for years, and live without almost any external condition that we recognise necessary for our happiness. You must have often questioned why people with so much are so unhappy while others with nothing are happy? It concludes that fame, money, friends, and all the external things never cause happiness—then what does cause happiness? However, if you understand one simple fact, it is not such a mystery, and the fact is—we live in our inner world more than we do in the external world.

From one perspective, life is transient, but it is an eternal existence that will remain forever. For the ignorant, life is transient, and death appears to be a reality. For an enlightened and conscious soul, life is eternal, and death is merely a lie. When people are not connected to their eternal selves, they want to prove their uniqueness and how special they are. Although they want peace, they don't give up the cause of restlessness. Though they want God, they fail to destroy their ego. They don't want to let go of their false identity, obsessions, and beliefs, yet they want self-realisation. Peace surfaces only when they remove the cause of disquiet and make them free of all sorrow. If you are connected with your transient self only, you often want to attract others' attention. The ignorant one also welcomes suffering and nourishes his ego, even if that doesn't make him happy. Awakening and being connected to the eternal self can also cure one of these diseases. Our ego is a disease itself that seeks something unique. It never gets satisfied with the ordinary. Ego makes you struggle, stress, and spend sleepless nights to possess something that you desire fervently, but the moment you get it, you see nothing special in it. This constantly makes you feel dissatisfied and unsuccessful.

According to Bernard Shaw, there are two types of suffering in the world. One is when you fail to get what you desire, and the other is when you get what you desire. The second is more destructive since it has no remedy. People who can understand this mind game believe in a remedy for such suffering. According to masters and gurus, one who gives up their desire to become special becomes truly special. Like other people, we also question why there is so much suffering in the world? But in reality, people create suffering from their ignorance and false beliefs about their true nature. The true self, the eternal self, is an ocean of bliss. If you live near your eternal self and connect with actual means, you can experience peace, equanimity, and happiness.

On the contrary, you might keep oscillating between likes and dislikes if you live away from your eternal self and are connected only with your transient self.

The circumstances and the world are judged based on the person's inner state. With a transformed and elevated vision, your perception would not see any sorrow or injustice. This world would appear just like a canvas to you. Your beliefs will paint hell and heaven on it, and your inner state will fill the colours. You are liberated when your painting stops. You perceive and create neither sorrow nor joy, for you have attained eternal peace through solid bondage with your infinite self. Our beliefs train our mind, and it sees and experiences only what it believes in. It possesses tremendous power. The entanglements of this life are what already your mind has perceived to be true. The world does not appear full of joy or suffering as you progress and mature. All such notions and perceptions stop at the end of the journey, and once you get connected with your eternal self, you manifest the steady-state of abidance in the 'Self.'

Focusing On the True Nature of "I"

Focusing on your true self has always been a dilemma as it requires changing the state of mind, the beliefs, and the foundational aspects of one's identity. Focusing on your true nature is not merely about getting to know yourself but rather knowing one self's depths. Some people even consider the act as mean and selfish. But in contrast, focusing on your true self is self-love, which each of you should master given the miseries the present world puts forth. When you have developed the habit of focusing on others, it gets hard for you to shift the gears. Concentrate on yourself; the "I" in me is about developing consciousness of your inner world and what it needs and desires to enlighten your mind. In today's developed world, focusing on your true self is also recognised through advanced practises of self-inquiry, which are often reserved for spiritually mature entities. Meditation has been practiced for ages to confront the true self and know and satisfy the soul's needs.

> "*True self is non-self, the awareness that the self is made only of non-self-elements. There's no separation between self and other, and everything is interconnected. Once you are aware of that, you are no longer caught in the idea that you are a separate entity.*"
>
> – Thich Nhat Hanh

Identification of the eternal self is as difficult as exposing it to others. Once, with practise, you can identify and recognise your true self, now is the time to expose it to the world. It is the exposure of your introspective, spiritual, conscious self that intends to harbour and spread harmony, balance, and joy. You are equally influenced by your eternal self as influenced by your transient self. Similarly, you can cast your influence on others. Also, it is essential to understand the true nature of the body and mind. Only then will we be able to identify "I" within me. The body and mind are two facets. Balancing both aspects can help in identifying the true nature of one's self.

The process is not as simple as it sounds. You need to develop an attitude where you subject your actions and thoughts to critique, analyse the responsive behaviours, and identify the patterns that can improve the overall being. You need to approach consciousness as much as you can. Consciousness, for many, is a slippery concept. It corresponds to the subjective experiences of people. For example, when you stub your toe, your brain doesn't merely process the information and trigger a reaction. Instead, you also experience a feeling of pain. In contrast, when you are happy, you feel joyful. The ethereal nature of the experience is the mystery at the heart of consciousness. Now the question is, how does the brain, a physical and concrete object, generate a nonphysical essence?

Focusing and knowing the true nature of self is also reflective of being conscious enough to pass the experiences while understanding their realities and staying calm. Why do we even want to know our true selves? What would happen if we neglect this part of our lives? There can be many answers to it, but the simplest response is that it brings us back into the beauty of each moment of our lives. Focusing on "I" and knowing your true self does not answer all your questions but makes them so much less important to ask. Once you attain true enlightenment by knowing your true self, it gives your life back with much deeper meanings. Your ego and daily life become more and more of an expression of who you truly are, who we all are, and what might be the purpose of our lives. The deeper the understanding, the compassionate the love would be, and you would attain blissful awareness. That's the "why" of knowing your true self.

Now the question is, how do you come to know your true self? What can you do to truly focus on "I"? Experts and meditators have devised many varied methods by various religious and cultural traditions. These multiple methods make it confusing which approach to adopt to reach the goal. But you must look for what makes each of them practical tools for knowing your true self and for enlightenment. Knowing this can help you utilise any religious or traditional practise more effectively. It can even help you avoid distractions of the cultural accidentals and orthodoxies and keep your focus fixed on the task of knowing your true self. In all these practises, the common element is the temporary suspension of discursive thinking. This makes them practical tools of enlightenment. So, what would discursive thinking do to our mind that it gets necessary for us to suspend it to know our true selves? It's just because discursive thinking is the life-blood of the ego's activity. Once you can suspend your discursive thinking, you can begin to have consciously lived experiences in life without intrusion of ego. With ego suspended, we get the chance to know our true nature.

When you are looking for and focusing on your true self, there is nothing to create or fix but instead to uncover and discover. Any meditation practise you follow, such as simply being aware or conscious breathing, would give you lived experience of being conscious without the activity of the ego. As you grow with this consciousness, you begin to know yourself without ego's activity, allowing yourself to have consciously lived experiences of your true nature. This process weakens your attachment with your ego over time.

Other People's Influences Form a Person's Existence

It's not only about how the true nature perceives the concepts, events, people, and patterns but also about the influences of other people giving rise to one's existence. For example, our perception of water is that it's an element that hydrates us and helps our body function appropriately. Our perception about water is what makes it water and not milk. Similarly, in a diverse society, different people hold different perceptions, to which the society subjects them. For example, in advanced and elite social classes, a psychiatrist is recognised as a medical expert who deals with mental health illnesses and cures patients with such illnesses. On the contrary, in middle and conservative communities and societies, the same psychiatrist is stereotyped with the notion that he tackles madness—two perceptions about one profession, a confusing state that creates further paranoia.

Other people influence the existence of a being. The influences of other people affect our reality. This might be due to the differences in opinions, perspectives, and different beliefs they hold. One factor that influences how you perceive others is the current cognitive accessibility of given person characteristics. That refers to the extent to which a person easily and quickly comes to mind for the perceiver. These differences in accessibility significantly influence the impressions you form about others because they influence what you focus on and how you think about them. For example, if you care a lot about fashion, you will describe the other person on the dimensions of style. These perception differences reflect and emphasise that we as observers place on the characteristics of others rather than the real difference between those people. As a result, our view of others may sometimes be more about ourselves than about them.

This reflects that other people's thoughts significantly influence our existence and perceptions, and the same goes for our perceptions and beliefs about other people. If the collective perception of people about others is harmonious and pleasing, it can bring peace on a community level. However, our consciousness is also influenced by perceptions about others and the environment surrounding us.

> "*The life of inner peace, being harmonious and without stress, is the easiest type of existence.*"
>
> – Norman Vincent Peale

Our existence is not merely the physical body and mind, relying on food and water, but also contains a soul that is the only guide to knowing the true self. The conscious being and soul are crucial components of the existence of human beings. They cannot be explained on the material science plane. One has the idea of the core of true self and presence of existence, relying on different aspects of life, can understand the reality behind the influences of other people. It is also necessary to identify someone's current state correctly and make opinions about them based on that understanding. It can help promote emotional intelligence in a person utilising consciousness as the tool of knowing and learning others.

Existence Has Multiple Parts

Existence is not merely the presence of beings living and surviving on Earth. Existence is not about a material body that survives for a specific time, dies, and decays. Instead, existence is the presence of three primary and critical parts; the body, the mind, and the energy. Dr Ted Hill, physician and a United Methodist, states, "We think of our lives as silos. But the body, mind, and spirit are interconnected, not separate." Our body is nothing but the accumulation of earth elements. When we say earth element, it does not mean planet Earth, but all those aspects of our existence are gross. This body is the grossest layer among all defined above; hence earth element has the abundance in making this body. Most gross objects carry all five senses: sight, sound, smell, touch, and taste. The sense is worthless if we can't experience the outward world. Sense of view is relevant only if there is something to see. This sense of sight matters most for the element of earth. This is why our brain can capture 80% of the data through the eyes.

Contrary to the body, the mind is a superior entity that imparts intellect in daily life activities and is crucial. The mind plays a vital role in setting up our experience. Our thoughts and emotions are other layers of existence. There is a great advantage to being human. We are equipped with our intelligence and can become aware of our body, mind, and energy at any moment with superior consciousness. Hence, we can become aware of our actions. It is essential to calm to the mind and body to make the most of this outside world.

Mind is also known as Manas in Sanskrit. This is something that separates human beings from animals. Animals lack the intellect to utilise the past impression of their experiences. This is where humans take a giant leap in the chain of evolution. We often confuse our mind with our brain. But they are poles apart. The brain is the physical organ in your body. While the mind is neither visible nor audible, neither can it be tasted, smelt, or touched, but we can experience our mind every moment. Mind is the body where thoughts are born, and our body reacts to those thoughts. There is always chatter in our brain, which is the result of our mind. The mind always keeps talking about our mistakes, mischief, guilt, self-criticism, rejection, jealousy, loneliness, insult, failure in the past, apprehension, fear, insecurity, anxiety, worry, concern, and nervousness about the future. It is never quiet. It keeps talking always. Our evolution until this age is also a result of our minds expanding and acquiring more intellect over the years.

Energy is the critical component of our existence that sustains life. Energy growth is directly linked to the well-being and prosperity of human existence. Sustaining a positive energy aura is taught by the majority of healers and meditators. When our mind experiences the soul, there are no more experiences of life that are remained for a reason. The source of soul and life energy is the same. Energy is the centre of the complex interplay between the mind and the body. We now know that matter in any form is energy. Energy continually moves from one part to another part of the body. The energy levels of the body influence the state of our mind. Not only this, but the energy we endure is also essential to keep an aura around that either promotes and attracts positive or negative. Energy transfer is real, and with positive core energy, influence can be made in life events and experiences. Our existence depends on these three critical components while being influenced by several elements. Most of the time, the core focus of presence in the majority is to find happiness in every aspect of life, for which at times, the soul is neglected and material is attracted more and more.

Happiness Is Misunderstood

Happiness is often misunderstood. Have you ever thought about what makes you happy? What are the specific conditions that make you more comfortable in life and which make you feel joyful? Our most significant misunderstanding is; happiness is something to be pursued. We think that happiness is conditional, and we have to go out there and get it. Well, that is only one way of living and not precisely what defines happiness with actual means. Our physical existence is tricked often, and we try to manufacture happiness from external stuff. Many others want to enhance their happy state through drugs, booze, sex, etc. For some people, one path to happiness is through specific, concrete goals of benevolence, such as by making someone smile, saving the environment, or making someone happy. Happiness is also the presence of positive emotions and the absence of negative ones. But happiness is something more than developing positive feelings. Instead, happiness is the joy one feels, an emotional state characterised by contentment, joy, satisfaction, and fulfilment.

> "*The happiness of your life depends upon the quality of your thoughts: therefore, guard accordingly, and take care that you entertain no notions unsuitable to virtue and reasonable nature.*"
>
> – Marcus Aurelius

When talking about happiness, most people talk about the joy they feel in the moment or might be referring to a more general sense of how they think about life overall. The balance of emotions and life satisfaction are recognised as the two key components of happiness. Each of us experiences positive and negative emotions, moods, and feelings. Happiness is linked with the positive energy and peace you create around yourself, attracting what it is made of. Once you can enlighten your true self, it becomes easy to avoid negative energy and keep a happy and positive aura around yourself.

Life satisfaction, on the other hand, makes you feel contented with what you have. You are contented with your achievements, relationships, job, etc. These feelings of satisfaction create a sense of bliss for you and draw you towards the positive aspects of life. You care less about what you don't have and focus on what you are blessed with. Our existence is dependent on happiness, too, to survive peacefully.

CHAPTER 3
THE BODY AND THE ACTION

Body and Mind, Separate or Inseparable?

We most often come across questions like if the mind is a part of the body, or is the body a part of the mind? Which of the two is in charge? If they are distinct, then how do they interact? We know that the mind is about mental processes, consciousness, and thoughts. The body, on the contrary, is about physical aspects of the brain neurons and how the brain is structured. Philosophers and scientists have presented many theories to explain the relationship between what we call your brain (i.e., part of your body) and your mind (defined as the conscious thinking 'you' experiences your thoughts). From the studies, we also know that both body and mind are crucial for functioning normally. The concept of dualism states that humans are characterised as having both a body/brain (physical) and a mind (nonphysical). Human beings are material objects. We characterise the materials around and within us through the indicators or values like solidity, weight, and various states of matter such as solids, liquids, and gases. However, unlike other material objects such as rocks, humans also possess the capability to form judgements and reason their existence. In short, they form the judgements and reasons through their mind. Dualism thus pertains to the view that the mind and the body both exist as separate entities. Descartes argues on dualism that there is a two-way interaction between mental and physical substances. He argued that the interaction of the mind with the body is through the pineal gland. This form of duality or dualism proposes that our mind controls the body. Still, the body also can influence the otherwise rational mind, such as when people act out of passion. Psychology also presents contrasting views about whether our mind or body are separate or related.

> *"To think about our bodies as horses to be ridden or even temples to be occupied, is to create a duality between our thinking and our body."*
>
> – Laurence Galian

The link between the mind and body can be depicted through an example. If your mind and its states, such as your desires and beliefs, are casually isolated from your bodily behaviour, then what goes on in your mind could not explain what you do. Thus, when separated, both body and mind are of no use as neither of them would project a healthy human consciousness or behaviour. You must have experienced the no-mind situation in your life. In fact, we experience it every day. Every day when we sleep, we are free from all kinds of distress and sorrow—a situation when any experience of our mind doesn't bother us with our problems. But the problem is when we wake up, they all come back again. Our efforts are in the direction to attain the no-mind in our waking state. We experience the whole world. We may indulge in our day-to-day life, job, family, and all other aspects of our lives, yet we will not get attached to the result of our actions.

Nowadays, youngsters take drugs to attain that state, but there is nothing more detrimental than this. It will negatively impact the body and brain. When the body is not ready for a conscious-no-mind, and we force it to attain such a situation, we cannot do detrimental things to our body. We should practise every day to reach a state where our bodies can sustain the changes. Slowly and gradually, we attain a situation where we can train ourselves to switch off the signal coming from our minds. It may happen any time and any place. Research says that you can create a new habit if you do something continuously for 21 days. But it is difficult to leave our old habits. A no-mind situation is great to overcome any unhealthy habit. It should be up to us to take help from the experience that we have attained from our mind or when the experience is not good then the priority is different.

It is essential to understand that we have control over our conscious mind, and our body acts in the direction our mind focuses on. While thinking about the connection between mind and body, the word connection implies two separate entities that function together to make a whole, conscious, living person. Followers of dualism consider there is no connection between mind and body, and they are the same. But these sorts of perspectives would not go far. Anything or everything that affects the mind also affects the body and vice versa. This is because the body lives in the mind, and the mind lives in the body. Whatever you focus your mind on, your body will follow direction. Also, the mind is the centre point of all the humanly conscious being, and its effort to align with the universal laws are guiding the body to follow the principles of harmonious living.

The connection and inseparability of body and mind can be made further comprehensive with specific examples. One belief regarding this connection is that our thoughts, beliefs, feelings, and attitudes can negatively or positively affect our biological functioning. In simpler words, our mind can affect how healthy our bodies are. This is not something new, as science has proven the effects of psychological wellbeing on the physiological well-being of a person. On the other hand, our mental state is impacted by what we do with our physical bodies, i.e., what we eat, how we walk and sit, and how much we exercise. Even our posture can affect our mental state positively or negatively. These aspects result in a complex interrelationship between our bodies and mind.

For example, suppose your workplace has provided you with uncomfortable chairs, which have led to back pain, further propagating it to restlessness and fatigue. Anything that enters the field of awareness of your body also affects your mental state. If you fix your back pain, the chances are that you can improve your problem-solving skills. If you make yourself more active, chances are you can sky-rocket your creativity. Everything we do, even reading this section of the book, is an altogether mind-body work; if one of them shuts, the other will not continue.

> *"Your entire body is like one big hologram. Each aspect is interrelated to other aspects of yourself."*
>
> – Catherine Carrigan

Another example we can take is from healthcare. So many of us believe in that involvement of the mental state in bodily ailments. However, even some mental health conditions can be remedied by changes in the body. For example, it has now been proven that exercise is the best tool to fight depression. The exercise starts a cascade of biological events that result in many health benefits for the body, including improved sleep, regulation of blood pressure, and heartbeat. Also, it improves mental state and mood by releasing the body's feel-good chemicals called endorphins. Exercise is an exclusive bodily movement, but it tends to impact the mind positively. On the contrary, physical ailments, such as cancer, negatively affect the mind. It leaves the person feeling depressed, less interested in daily activities, and less social.

Take the example of athletes; how they train the body 100 per cent impacts what happens in the mind and how they prepare the mind 100 per cent impacts what happens in the body. During the training of athletes, the entire mind-body are counted. Would a distracted athlete learn a new skill or exert adequate effort optimally? No. Because he is not focused. Is an over-trained athlete going to thrive under pressure or think straight? Of course not. Because he has not been trained yet to keep and maintain the focus while putting in 100 per cent effort, the athletes are not counting the entire mind-body in both cases. Your body does what your mind asks and directs it towards. If you are not good mentally or have a bad mood day, you won't enjoy the moments and might find everything irritating you. For the body to act healthily, it requires our mind to work normally and optimally. Similarly, for the mind to work optimally, it requires our bodies to function healthily. The connection is even deeper when we elevate the states of consciousness. With elevated consciousness, one can even sense and feel the energies within and around. This can help in further strengthening the mind-body connection.

Body and The Action

The identity of anything in this universe is defined by how you experience the object or 'action.' There are two phenomena, first one: body Planets, stars, meteorite, the Earth, the moon—are all an example of the body which, when thought of separate from action, are nothing. However, when they are combined with the action, they become complete. It is true with each particle in the entire universe.

Let's take the example of our eyes! Eyes without action are nothing, but it becomes essential when they see the whole world. Similarly, the human body without any effort is nothing; when combined with a different action, it takes the form of the human body. A book is just a collection of pages, but when it is written on some subject or some theme, then it becomes interesting. Both object and action complement each other. They are not complete in one another's absence. All the actions such as creating a universe, revolving planet, and satellite talk about their state.

Similarly, objects on Earth such as stone, pen, paper have their action defining their current state. The same is the case with humans. The senses, organs, appendages are the body, and their capabilities to sense, function, and move is the action, keeping the human as a whole being with mind and spirit.

Everything in this illusionary world (Prakriti) consists of three natures (Gunas). These three qualities are present in all objects in nature, and among the three, one is always dominant. There can be only three types of actions in the entire universe based on these three qualities. All three actions work together. These actions are Tamas (Frenziness), Rajas (Continuity), Sattva (Stillness). Although, Sattva, Rajas and Tamas are the Gunas (qualities), they may sound like action to many. Due to these Gunas (qualities), action can be decided. Each action displays either of the three Gunas and depicts the Guna which is dominant over all. Our actions are based on these Gunas and so is our behaviour. Gunas are present in everything; humans, food, animate and innate objects. As human beings, we can consciously change the levels of Gunas in our minds and bodies. We can increase or decrease the Gunas by altering the influence and presence of lifestyle, external objects, and thoughts. The dominant Guna will affect how we perceive life around us. It will affect the attitude, behaviour, attachments, actions, and so on.

Three Qualities of Nature

Following are three types of actions:

1. Tamas (Frenziness) – It is also called inertia. The attribute or quality of inertia, ignorance, darkness, heaviness, doubt, slow-moving, dense, sloth, laziness, lassitude, dullness, sleep, inadvertence, and stupidity all fall in this category. Also, Tamas is related to the earth element. This is where we create our habits. It is associated with inertia in life. This also induces dullness, laziness, lethargy, too much affinity with food, and wandering. Ideally, this quality of nature is nothing but how primitive humans lived. Animals fall in this category. They all bother about two things: food and reproduction. This is also related to only survival. Among us, there is an animal that wants to suppress others growth. The lower three energy points are associated with this quality of nature. We will see this in detail when dealing with the energy body in later chapters.

2. Rajas (Continuity) - Our emotions need to flow continuously. Love, attraction, working on a project and not showing any lethargy, connecting with family and friends all fall under this quality. Trying to grow and not pulling someone down or making others terrible is part of striving for success. Anything that requires continuous action is required (not as inertia but as a part of creativity) is called continuity.
3. Sattva (Stillness) - We reduce our speed not because of lethargy but because of observing the most minor incident happening within and around us; we will see things changing continuously. Slowly and gradually, it will take us to the point where we can experience any changes in the cosmos. As we increase this "quality of nature," cosmic intelligence unfolds. We know what, when, and how to respond to any incident outside us. So, we keep our calm always as we experience eternal peace as we go slow and experience complete stillness. Stillness—in terms of thoughts—minimal thought. i.e., Moving your mind to delta state (Ref chap: cosmic intelligence—the brain). Stillness—in terms of action. Be aware of all conscious effort and observe the minutest change in the subconscious action such as heartbeat, blood flow, digestion, tingling sensation in the body, scratching urge on the face, and any other part of the body. Stillness provides the patience and power to observe the changing moment.

> *"The three Gunas [qualities] happen: Sattva, rajas, and tamas. These three Gunas come in cycles into our life. When Sattva comes, there is alertness, knowledge, interest, joy, happiness—everything comes. When rajoguna comes, there is more desire, feverishness, restlessness and sadness. When tamoguna comes—delusion, attachment, lack of knowledge, lethargy—all these come."*
>
> – Sri Sri Ravi Shankar

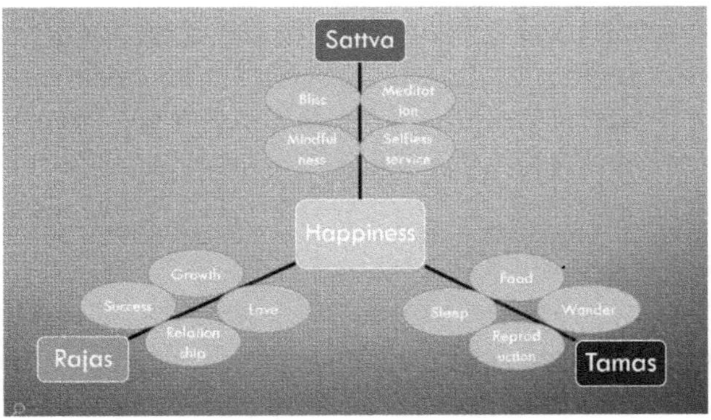

All three states are always present within us, and our nature is decided by the nature we possess in excess. Our aim should be to increase the stillness to unlock cosmic intelligence. Several practises are related to our body, mind, and energy, which will move us from the lower state to the higher state. As we grow and mature, we tend to understand how our happiness relies on nature and how it alters with changes in nature. For example, as you become kinder and humble, you find joy in developing positive relationships and certain habits or activities that make people around you happy. Happiness is the state of mind that we attain either by our actions or environmental influences. It is, however, never static and constantly changing states. One can attain happiness in all three qualities of nature, but happiness might be different for different people. For example, a person with dominant Tamas would feel happy while having food of their choice. A person with Rajas as the dominant quality of their nature would feel happy by accumulation and expansion. A person with Sattva, as the dominant quality of their nature, would feel happy by understanding minute observable aspects of his well-being and expanding their cosmic intelligence.

Sattva and Cosmic Intelligence

Nature consists of these three Gunas or primal qualities, which are the main powers of Cosmic intelligence that determine your spiritual growth. According to Yoga and Ayurveda, all objects in the universe consist of these three Gunas. Moreover, the process of cosmic evolution consists of the mutual interaction between the three Gunas and their transformation.

Of all the three Gunas, it is Sattva through which one can achieve the ascensions of cosmic intelligence. Sattva, in origin, is a Sanskrit word that means harmony, pure essence, and light. In its wider meanings, it also represents creative potential, intelligence, and equilibrium. The essential elements or qualities one might need to adopt to develop and expand their cosmic intelligence. Sattva can only be renewed in space and silence. It is worn out by excessive mental activity, including excessive philosophical or intellectual thinking. Currently, most of our relaxation today involves TV, entertainment, and screens of any kind.

When you perform Sattvic healing, you are using nature, the life force, and the power of the cosmic mind. When you perform Sattvic healing, you perform treatment through a vegetarian diet, herbs, meditation, and mantra. Rajas are infrequently used for the healing process. Sattva, being a condition of harmony, is always used for healing purposes. Why Sattva is linked with cosmic intelligence is because it brings cosmic harmony. The cosmic intelligence potentially holds Sattva predominantly, with a little of Rajas and Tamas[2]. Sattva brings cosmic harmony and promotes the development and expansion of cosmic intelligence. With enlightened Sattva, you are at peace and harmony inside out, and you can feel your life aligned with universal patterns. Further, Sattva-driven cosmic intelligence also enables you to use the universal laws and principles to perform healing and to ensure your spiritual growth.

Types of Actions in Three Gunas

Corresponding to the three Gunas are the three qualities of nature. Although these qualities have been discussed earlier, their link with happiness has yet to be established. Moreover, the type of actions in each of

2 Iyengar, B. K. S. (2008). *AstadalaYogamala (Collected Works), Volume 8* (Vol. 1). Allied Publishers.

the Gunas is also important to be discussed as they are linked with different types of happiness one feels. The Gunas can even be used to describe different types of happiness. Happiness that comes from selfless, sattvic knowledge is the hardest to achieve. At first, it will feel bitter to work without any thought of personal gain. However, this happiness is the only path to real and permanent happiness. When you are truly a Sattvic person, your intentions and actions are different from others. A truly Sattvic person is pure in thoughts, has mental clarity, and clear words and actions. They are not lethargic or lazy. They don't overwork or push in life but enjoy a balanced life. The key to having Sattvic life is cultivating little by little, cultivating Sattva daily by what we eat, how we think, move, practise, and speak. Sattvic actions are natural both in their cultivation and their essence.

Contrary to Sattva, Rajas knowledge is selfish, and so are their actions. It barely sees the unity in everything and considers different things and creatures as separate entities. Rajasic intellect fails to tell right from wrong because it lacks this crucial understanding harboured by Sattva. Rajas actions pursue pleasure, wealth, and good reputation often at the expense of others. Happiness that comes from Rajas actions and intentions is pleasurable and immediate but temporary. It is the joy of getting something you have always wanted, such as the thrill of eating spicy food. The bad thing is, such happiness fades quickly and reveals itself to be an illusion.

In the case of Tamas, such knowledge is deduced—like a child. It sees one part of the world and thinks that's all there is and lacks the vision that there might be something beyond its own experiences. Such knowledge mixes right and wrong at every turn. Tamasic actions lead to grief, fear, refusal, and sadness and make a person learn from their mistakes. Happiness embraced from Tamasic actions is a lie from beginning to end. This false happiness must be avoided.

Only with Sattvic knowledge, actions, and intentions can we achieve ultimate happiness—the happiness of "I," which is eternally present and blissful. We all want to be happy from the depths of our hearts yet we fail to achieve that ultimate happiness. We surrender "I" before Tamasic and Rajasic actions and intentions which bring temporary and unreal happiness. The fact that our happiness and suffering are insignificant compared to other living beings must also be considered while approaching ultimate and eternal happiness. Considering the misery others are experiencing increases the sense of gratitude which brings immense happiness. For ultimate happiness, we must ask ourselves what we consider most important—what do we wish for, daydream about, or strive for? For some people, worldly happiness is their ultimate happiness, such as material possession, a large house with luxuries, a well-paid job, a fast car. For others, happiness lies in reputation, adventure, good looks, and excitement. This is due to the dominance of one of the three qualities of nature: Rajas, Tamas, and Sattva. Many try to find the meaning of their life and happiness in relationships with their family and friends. All these things can make one happy for a short while, but they can also cause suffering and worry. Such aspects never give us the perfect lasting happiness that we long for in our hearts. Worldly attainments are hollow and are not the real essence of human life.

From my perspective, the only thing that will never deceive us that will provide our eternal happiness is the attainment of full enlightenment. Whether you achieve it via Sattva, cosmic intelligence, meditation, yoga, or anything, you must ensure that you have fully attained enlightenment. By enlightenment, I mean omniscient wisdom free from all mistaken appearances. A person who possesses this wisdom can be recognised as an enlightened being.

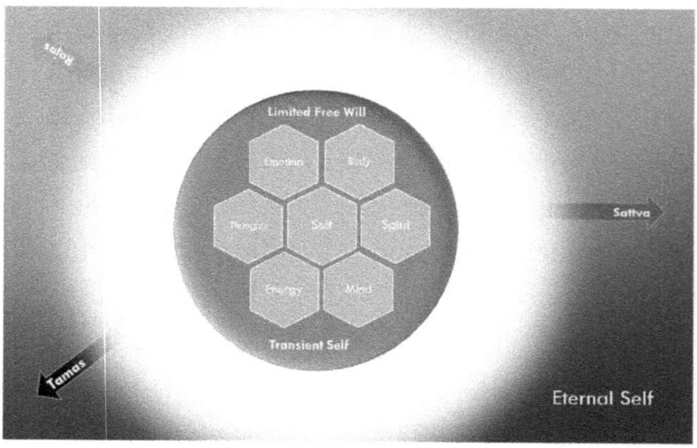

Once you can achieve complete enlightenment, you understand the concept of free will. Our free wills are limited, and a person understanding the underpinned concept holds the potential to control their emotions, energy, thoughts, mind, spirit, body, and overall self. This is what Sattva teaches, and Sattvic actions are based on. Once understood, the concept of free will enables you to embrace Sattvic actions and intentions for your life, automatically leading you to eternal happiness that your soul yearns for. Many people think that their worldly possessions will make them happy forever. In contrast, an enlightened person knows that these possessions are temporary and the happiness imparted by them would not last forever.

Cosmos Provides the Intelligence

I have realised it myself so many times; when you ask from the cosmos, you affirm and realise that it has already happened to you. You need to sit back and wait for your dream to be realised. Then, someone or something will give you a sign that is so subtle that you need to realise and pay attention, and you will understand what this cosmos wants from you. I see 747 all the time in the last four years. Divine guidance may come from the traffic, family member, friend, enemy, colour, and everything you come across. It may come in the dead of night. Recognising and realising is where you start the process of developing cosmic intelligence. The more you respond to the signals, your cosmic intelligence becomes stronger and more stable. From my experiences, cosmos, if consciously embraced, not only helps you understand your life dilemmas but also imparts you with the knowledge of how to deal with these dilemmas in the most efficient ways.

It also relies on our control of the subconscious mind. Psychologists now state that 95% of our thoughts and behaviour come from the subconscious mind and 5% from the conscious mind[3]. The activities controlled by the subconscious include personality, body function, long-term memory, creativity, patterns, emotions, beliefs and values, and habits. So, if you can control your subconscious mind, you can control these actions, behaviours, and overall personality traits.

> *"Everything is within your power, and your power is within you."*
>
> – Janice Trachtman

When we pay attention to the conscious awareness inside ourselves, a crucial realisation that we can find easily is that we neither separate from other people nor from the universe itself as we seem to be. Human life can be recognised as a continuous stream of transient moments, and when we pay attention to the past or the future, we drift away from consciously being present here at the moment, here and now. At times, our thoughts about ourselves and our life become the focus of attention, and we forget to pay attention to the consciousness inside us occasionally. Our conscious and subconscious are just quietly experiencing everything, including the influences of the cosmos. The conscious cosmic space within us helps us realise and know the extent of cosmic intelligence we possess, the conscious

---

3 Mahoney, M., (2003). The Subconscious Mind of the Consumer (And How to Reach It). https://hbswk.hbs.edu/item/the-subconscious-mind-of-the-consumer-and-how-to-reach-it

awareness, and what has been missing in our conscious mind that can expand this intelligence. Attending and focusing inward helps in dissolving the thought boundaries and realisation of a thought-free inner space. Moreover, it helps rediscover our intuitive connection with the Divine. These extremes of realisation are driven by a cosmic intelligence, which brings all life into our beings throughout the universe.

Each of us possesses an unlimited, infinite cosmic intelligence transforming itself into the living form of a human being for the duration of human life. In our true nature, we are cosmic beings, and expressions of cosmic intelligence exist within our conscious and subconscious inner space. If we take hold, we can access the transformative power of this intelligence whenever we choose. With the power and controlled cosmic intelligence in our beings, we can tune into an infinite consciousness with unlimited capacity for change and evolution.

> *"The mind is not limited to the thoughts and imagination, but your mind is part of the cosmos of the universe. Your mind is your whole awareness field."*
>
> – Roshan Sharma

CHAPTER 4
THE BODY

"Destruction, hence, like creation, is one of Nature's mandates."
– Marquis de Sade

Destruction and Formation - Nature of the Cosmos

As the planets and stars move around some centre of reference, they all are bound to move under the effect of one another. If one system of stars gets destroyed, it gives birth to many other small planetary systems, meteorites, and other heavenly objects. So, destruction and creation are continuous processes of the cosmos. Again, small particles come together to create supernova, and hence larger objects come into being. These patterns follow the first law of thermodynamics, also called the Law of Conservation of Energy. It states, energy can neither be created nor destroyed; energy can only be transferred or changed from one form to another.

> *"Modern physics has... revealed that every sub-atomic particle not only performs an energy dance but also is an energy dance; a pulsating process of creation and destruction."*
>
> – Fritjof Capra

Our universe began with an explosion of space itself—the Big Bang—the mega-destruction event that led to the origin or beginning of the universe's formation. It all started with extremely high temperature, density, and the simplest elements formed. The matter was later drawn together by gravity to form the first stars and the first galaxies. Our universe has been expanding since its beginning. Though we don't feel it, yet it's happening. One can get the idea from the Big Bang Theory that destruction is necessary for formation. To keep existence going, every particle in this world has the power to expand itself. The smallest molecule joins to make a bigger molecule. Bigger molecules join to make a particle, and so on. As gravity drew the matter together, galaxies collected into groups, clusters, and superclusters. During this process, several stars die in supernova explosions, and the chemical remnants of which seeded new generations of stars and led to the formation of rocky planets. Life evolved to consciousness on at least one such planet.

Cosmic cycles have a long tradition in religion and philosophy. Several cultures have embraced the idea of time as an ever-turning wheel. Ancient people imagined that a cosmic 'spring' would follow each cosmic 'winter' in a perpetual sequence of phases, just as the seasons on the Earth.

Many people became attached to us the moment we exist on this planet. The closest are our mother and father. They contribute to shaping us as with their knowledge and understanding based on their life experiences. We are raised against our will till a certain age. Then, slowly and gradually, we make sense of our surroundings. We observe our family members and relatives closely. This is when we discover that our mother and father teach something and practise something else. Sub-consciously we feel deceived. We see them fighting, screaming, sometimes lying to other adults, ignoring their work, not keeping their promises with other adults, and so on.

These activities don't happen as per our wish, but still, we must go through it. We start making sense of religious faith, political belief, and social connection due to discussion around us. Our belief system is not made as per our wishes. External sources are working to make our belief system. Having seen this, we start making our reality and truth repeatedly. In the meantime, we find that when we cry, the next person, our mom, doesn't feel good and does all possible things to make us happy. When in pain, the father tries all possible things to make that pain go away. On this foundation, we start building our emotions. All these sources are external, but the impact is internal. We begin developing these emotions again without our own will. As a kid, we develop a sense and think about the family, society, religion, politics, finances, relationships, and it all happens without asking any permission from ourselves. All these things happen naturally.

The day my elder son was born, an obstetrician met with an accident. As a result, the delivery process didn't go so well, and he was grunting at the time of birth. I had to take him to another hospital for better treatment. Unfortunately, the doctors were not very encouraged with his situation. At that moment, I thought, how come he could go under multiple diagnoses, so many needles penetrating him from his head to toe. I still remember when my wife saw him for the first time, we both broke down in the hospital and cried after seeing him on a ventilator. Everything should have been well if the obstetrician had not met with an accident. But now, when I see him, I feel proud of him.

Let's start with our childhood. In childhood, our parents give us toys and teach us to share with others. When a mischievous boy comes to our house, he destroys all the toys. That is the first instance we see ourselves as helpless, feel pain, and then blackmailing them for all sorts of big and small issues. We understand that the person who is our father will feel bad if we get hurt. So, we start blackmailing that person by hurting ourselves, sometimes physically, other times verbally, and saying mean things about ourselves. Later, when we grow up, we find that things are not working out, and we take another step to get our wish accomplished. We start hurting others physically, mentally, and emotionally, by any means to feel the pleasure we are missing out on. We don't leave any stone unturned to get our things done. It becomes a part of our personality, and after sometime, we feel proud by saying that we can make others work. Later, we are rewarded by the organisation/company we work for.

This is how we start believing that we are the hero of our lives and can make things happen as per our wishes. With our worldly achievements and accomplishments, we become our role models. However, our growing age later antagonises our success and achievements. In our childhood, we are weak, and with growing age, we reach adulthood, and have strong bodies and bones. At this age, most of us go after efforts for successful life, stability, and future. However, after few years, when the body again becomes weak, our health deteriorates, and our wish will have little significance in our lives. Our growing age makes it easy to understand what things are essential and what should be focused on. We follow this universal pattern because our existence is relying on universal and cosmic patterns.

Life without the revolution of the moon is not possible. This can be proven by scientific evidence. The median duration of a singleton pregnancy following conception is 265 days, equivalent to nine synodic months. Also, the menstrual cycle has a mean duration of 28 days, although there may be variations (one synodic month). Since ancient times, this has led to the belief that there is a link between fertility, moon, conception, and childbirth[4]. When the mother's body aligns with the moon's revolution cycle around the Earth, it can come

4 Morales-Luengo, F., Salamanca-Zarzuela, B., Urueña, S. M., García, C. E., &Carboner, S. C. (2020). External influences on birth deliveries: Lunar gravitational and meteorological effects. *Anales de Pediatría (English Edition), 93*(6), 367-373.

into existence. We take birth at a particular time when the planets and stars form specific combinations in the cosmos. The impact of this specific time and position of the planets and stars is always on the human body and mind throughout their life. All life is connected; all cosmos is connected. You are a part of the cosmos, and the cosmos is a part of you from birth. You cannot deny the reality that you depend on the cosmos for your life, birth, and existence.

We grow and evolve in the presence of the cosmos. Since childhood, we taught about the five senses—smell, sight, touch, taste, and hearing. We know how to use these senses even from a young age and investigate the world around us. We are born curious, but our senses do more than just identifying the world we live in. They serve beyond our perception, playing an integral role in emotional learning, processing, and interpretation. Both our emotions and senses are tightly intertwined. As our senses evolve, our emotions follow. What we hear, taste, see, smell, and touch can provide us with information on how to feel. In other words, what we feel can be heavily influenced by what our senses are taking in. As we grow, our personality evolves and develops. Based on different aspects, the seven fundamental traits of personality are;

- The way you behave,
- The way you feel,
- The way you learn and communicate,
- The way you relate to others,
- The way you get angry and how you manifest that,

- The way you are naturally successful in and,
- The way you are naturally challenged in.

Your personality acquires these seven traits and stands out uniquely among others. Your personality traits influence your characteristic patterns of feelings, thoughts, and behaviours. Moreover, personality traits imply stability and consistency. For example, someone who scores high in any particular trait such as extraversion is predicted to be sociable in different situations and over time. The psychology of traits thus rests on the idea that people differ from one another in terms of where they stand on a set of basic trait dimensions that persists across situations and over time. It is now known that personality tends to get better over time, and psychologists call it 'the maturity principle.' People, as they grow old, become more emotionally stable, extroverted, conscientious, and agreeable. These changes are often pronounced over the long haul.

> *"I think we all have our personality, unique and distinctive, and at the same time, I think that our own unique and distinctive personality blends with the wind, with the footsteps in the street, with the noises around the corner, and with the silence of memory, which is the great producer of ghosts."*
>
> – Octavio Paz.

The Ultimate Bliss

Is there really a secret to happiness? Is it really even possible to achieve ultimate bliss? How can we experience it in our lives with our physical bodies? Is ultimate bliss merely a concept of happiness or something beyond happiness? Is there any importance of our physical bodies in achieving ultimate bliss? How can we experience ultimate bliss with this physical body? These are some of the questions you must ask yourself while seeking ultimate bliss and being willing to achieve it with this intact physical body. Depending on the person involved, happiness can have a different meaning for different people. One can achieve ultimate bliss by mindfulness. Such people live in the present moment, being neither too anxious nor too calm. They are genuinely natural inside out. They are mindful of what they eat, drink and are aware of in the present. This is achievable when your body is well aware of the environment, your inside, your outside. To experience ultimate bliss, you must enjoy being in the present moment. Try enjoying your meals, showers, travels, and the first bite of gooey chocolate cake. For ultimate bliss, one must enjoy the beauty of the present instead of focusing on the past or future or multitasking. Appreciate the small, incredible things in life: manifest positivity, practise channelling energy. Meditation is one of the best ways by which one can practise mindfulness and achieve ultimate bliss. As you practise mindfulness, you present little retreats to your mind that keep your head away from all anxiety and stress that life brings.

> *"There is neither happiness nor unhappiness in this world; there is only the comparison of one state with another. Only a man who has felt ultimate despair is capable of feeling ultimate bliss."*
>
> – Alexandre Dumas

Not only meditation and mindfulness, but you must also learn emotional intelligence, the potential to be aware of your emotions and managing them accordingly. It would help if you accepted your emotions, as they are a part of your well-being. Achieving ultimate bliss requires you to be fully aware of your emotions and be in peace with them. Allow yourself to be sad, mourn, or be happy. Don't just bottle your emotions; recognise their worth for your well-being. Doing so will make you feel more conscious and aware of your emotions. People who accept their negative emotions are more content as compared to those denying their negative emotions. Even in some cases, most positive people experience sadness and negativity every once in a while, which is perfectly normal. Allow your mind and body to go through whatever life brings you.

Your body is the mirror of your soul. When you nourish your body, you clear your mind. Self-care is one of the most important aspects and easiest things on the list. Self-care is essentially a natural remedy for treating the conditions such as depression, anxiety, and stress. Have a spa day, the best stress reliever for your body. You don't need to visit a spa for self-care. We are a technology-oriented global society, and technology has facilitated us to have exotic experiences while staying at home. You can find many home alternatives for a spa day at home. For example, light some scented candles, fill your tub with warm water, and sip cucumber water. While doing so, read a book or listen to some soothing music. You are relaxing your body, your mind, and overall mental health. For a blissful life, a healthy work-life balance is also essential. You cannot be happy if you're overworked and don't have time for yourself. Your well-being also requires harmony and peace with relationships. Maintaining a work-life balance helps where you manage to spend quality time with your friends and family. Spending time with nature on weekends and meeting new people also helps in managing and sustaining healthy relationships. Nature has an immediate calming effect on your overall body and health.

One other important thing to keep in mind to attain ultimate bliss is avoiding contact with negative people. For example, people who complain about everything and appreciate nothing. Having negative people in your life adds to daily stress, primarily because you absorb their negative energy. By keeping a circle of negative people, you might be affecting your overall health and well-being. What's worse? You'll be attracting more negativity. Being around negative people doesn't make you feel good. It's not good for your mental and emotional well-being. Although the influences are not visible, they affect your positive energy and aura around you. Alongside avoiding contact with negative people, one must also free themselves from all the negativity in their thoughts and give space for positive thoughts.

All these practises are approachable and can lead to ultimate bliss. Most people consider ultimate bliss a form of ultimate happiness. To some extent, it is correct. A person who has achieved ultimate bliss appears the happiest person among many. However, ultimate bliss also imparts ultimate satisfaction, harmony, and peace within your internal and external world, joy in each moment, and no sign of irritation and agitation. A person who appears happy might not have all these or may have some. However, a person with ultimate bliss would certainly have these elements in their personality. One must also need to take care of your physical body to achieve ultimate bliss. Sound sleep, a stress-free routine, a healthy diet, and moderate exercise are helpful tips in keeping the body in the direction of attaining ultimate bliss.

Elements of Nature

This body or cosmic objects are made of the five elements. If you know how to organise these five elements properly, if you know how to keep these five elements within yourself, then there is nothing more to live in terms of health, wealth, well-being, perception, enlightenment. The five basic factors of existence and critical elements of nature, cosmos, and our bodies are; air, water, fire, earth, and ether. Though they all seem independent of each other, yet they are part of one another.

These five elements are related to our mind and body. According to Upnishadas, an ancient Hindu literature all the elements are originated from ether.

Ether moves to become air, air makes friction to become fire, as fire becomes denser, it condenses into water, and water becomes earth as it coagulates. All these five elements are contained in the earth. The Sanskrit words for these five elements are;

- Akasha (Ether)
- Vayu (Air)
- Tejas or Agni (Fire)
- Apas (Water)
- Prithvi (Earth)

> *"Don't dismiss the elements. Water soothes and heals. Air refreshes and revives. Earth grounds and holds. Fire is a burning reminder of our own will and creative power. Swallow their spells. There's a certain sweet comfort in knowing that you belong to them all."*
>
> – Victoria Erickson

A harmonious relationship between these five elements is necessary, which helps liberate our thought process to rekindle the mind-body connection. A harmonious relationship between all the five elements is also necessary to attain ultimate bliss. Each person has a dominant element that influences their nature and personality traits. Without these five elements, we are nothing, as each is important for our survival on this planet. You must understand each element's positive and negative aspects to tune your mind to use each element in the most effective ways possible. The rule of thumb is, we cannot dominate these elements. Instead, we must surrender to them and respect them. Figuring out their essential characteristics and relation to physical attributes is the best way to grip these five elements. By doing so, you might also be capable of understanding the universal laws and using the knowledge to harness the energy of your dominant element.

Of all, the earth is the most powerful element. It is the source of stability, dominates the centre and diagonal directions, and represents balance. When your earth element is in a balanced state, you witness a balanced state as it induces the state of stability, harmony, and peace. When you strengthen your earth element, you enhance the strength of mind, determination, steadfastness, and uninterrupted advancement.

The water element is an enormous life force. It also has substantial healing powers with nurturing energies. Throughout the planet, one can witness perfect cycles of water. Water has the potential to pull out negativity, making our minds calm and focused, and balancing the emotions.

Behind all life processes, fire is the driving force. Fire induces confidence, power, fame, money, and recognition when in a balanced state. The fire element is also recognised as the element of love and is all related to the heart. It represents our relationships with ourselves as well as with others. When individuals have balanced fire elements, they are often perceptive, clear, and discriminating judgment. They can digest as well as synthesise large amounts of information.

The air element represents our most basic connection to life. We can survive only when we breathe. Air represents growth and is associated with joy, movement, happiness. Air induces courage and perseverance when in a balanced state and makes you achieve your goals.

Ether or space represents enhancement or expansion. A balanced state induces awareness and knowledge and makes the person understand creative and new ideas. The space element influences the mind and heart and encompasses everything around. When you learn to strengthen and enhance your space element, you smoothly sync your energies with universal ones.

Each of these five elements is important for mind, body, and soul, and their balancing. A person capable of harnessing the energies of their birth element is better able to understand the criticalities of life and the wisdom behind events and overcome the challenges life throws at them.

> *"Be like the ancient elements in thinking. Like Earth, build upon a foundation of facts. Like air, be willing to change your ideas if the winds of evidence require it. Like fire, be unquenched in a desire for learning more. Like water, both our ideas and the tides can be unstoppable."*
>
> – C.A.A. Savastano

CHAPTER 5
THE ELEMENT

"The quality of your life depends on how well you manage your body, your mind, your emotion, your situations, your home, your communities, nations, your life in general and the world."

– Sadhguru

Essential Elements of Life

Our life is the product of our experiences, all the people we meet and all the relationships we form along the way. Even our mistakes and regrets are a part of ourselves. Throughout our lives, we connect with people, interact with them and sometimes these connections last for a lifetime. Since we open eyes in this world, we start making connections. Whether they are living things or non-living ones, we value them all in some way and this goes on until we die, so what do we really do in our lives? How can we decide if we have lived a fulfilled life? To lead a fulfilled life, an individual must first take care of their health. Take the example of, an unused machine in a factory which has stopped functioning; similarly, a body that remains inactive becomes weak and useless. Even though it's said that the body is just a container for our soul, we must remember that the soul will get lost if the container breaks.

"A healthy outside starts from the inside."
– Robert Urich

Thus, it's imperative that you take good care of your health by consuming a healthy diet. A human's body is approximately 72% water, hence it is advised that we should consume foods that have a water content of more than 70%, for example, vegetables. There are also fruits that are over 90% water. Many cultures, especially the Asian culture, has been developed throughout the course of time in such a way that it has emphasised on consuming more vegetables and fruits.

Then comes the factor of wealth. Wealth is crucial in today's world to sustain a life. An individual must be able to bear the daily expenses, whether it's food or clothing. It is the duty of an individual to provide themselves and their dependents with at least the bare necessities needed to survive. However, understand what wealth means to you, do you want bigger cars, a bigger house or are you also running in the marathon to earn more money to buy irrelevant material things. Nowadays, it's no more difficult to get lost in the pursuit of tangible things and forget things that are the most important in your life like your family, children, and your own mental peace, which is the third important factor.

How rich you are does not determine the quality of your life, instead you should focus on how happy you are or how peaceful do you feel with your life, as that's what gives life true meaning. Your well-being and mental peace are more important than some new electronic device. You must train yourself mentally and emotionally to lead a fulfilled life. A person who is not strong emotionally can easily be swayed by impurities in the outside world. It's your own self you need to control and manage, no one else has power to control you and you must not give anyone else this power. Leading to our fourth factor which is perception. Is the world is according to your perception. As Buddha said,

"Your mind is everything, what you think, you become."

Thus, you must always look at life with a positive outlook. If you think something is a certain way, it will manifest that way in your reality so you must always think positive and have an open mind. If you follow these factors, you'll be able to reach enlightenment. The real meaning behind enlightenment is not to know something nobody else knows, it's the control and power you feel over your own self. Thus, you are only enlightened when you are in control of all the aspects of your life. However, there's a deeper way, a thorough way to gain firm control over all the aspects of your life.

Five Fundamental Factors of Existence

To live a fulfilled life and gain true cosmic intelligence, we must make sure to focus on the five elements of existence. As I've said earlier, our existence is not only dependent on our body but a lot more. Every existence living or non-living is made of five elements also called the "Pancha Bhutas," which are:

1. Space
2. Air - Intellectual
3. Water - Emotional
4. Fire - Spiritual
5. Earth – Practical

Each of the five elements represent a state of matter. Earth doesn't just mean mud but everything that is liquid. Air is everything that is a gas but fire, fire is that part of nature that holds the power to transforms one state of matter into another. For example, fire transforms ice into steam. Many yogic and tantric rituals also worship fire as it is believed to purify and control other states of matter.

> *"This body is made of five fundamental elements—earth, water, fire, air, and space. The quality of your life essentially depends on how wonderful these five elements are within you."*
>
> – Sadhguru

These elements are the basis of creation. A human body is 72% Water, 12% is Earth, 6% Air, 4% Fire and the remaining 6% is Space[5]. Out of these five elements, you need not worry about Space if you just want to live well as Space is known as the mother of the all the other elements. The experience of space is the basis of a higher spiritual experience which is not in the domain of an ordinary person. Four elements are enough if you just want to live a full and content life. Out of these four elements, air is the easiest to manage and control because we breathe in air, and we can control our breathing patterns to control our heart rate, pulse, etc. These elements combine to become the foundation of life itself, and if you have even a small amount of mastery and control over any one of these elements inside of you, you'll start living a better more peaceful life.

In our mind, we believe all these elements to be independent of each other, however that is not true at all. If everything in this cosmos is connected, how can the basic elements of nature be disconnected from each other? Space is the root of all that exists. It represents that one element which is at the root of all and also is the cause of all other elements. If you take a look at the list once again, you might notice that the way the elements are arranged is not merely a coincidence. The elements are arranged to show that the element which comes first in the list causes the element which comes

5 Dallasyogafest, (2017). The 5 Elements of Nature and Their Relationship with The Human Body. https://dallasyogafest.org/2017/07/11/the-5-elements-of-nature-and-their-relationship-with-the-human-body/

below. That means, Earth element is caused by water, and water is caused by fire and hence fire is caused by air and air started due to space. Whereas, space was caused from nothingness as science also describes that it came to exist due to the Big Bang. Some elements are also seen as the enemy of the other, in a way that they block the expression of the other. For example, fire and water will "destroy" each other if they get too close. To co-exist, they must be separated. Too much fire in the body can create inflammation, whereas too much water can dampen fire and cause indigestion. On the other hand, some elements are said to "love" each other in a way that they are supportive and nurturing and enhance each other. Earth and water co-exist peacefully and are said to "hug" each other, and air and fire escalate each other. Other elements are simply termed as friendly and cooperative as they can live together without problems.

All these elements are present within us. The most common knowledge being that human beings are 72% water. Our body is made of different elements, each forming different structures. Solid structures, for example, bones, flesh, skin, tissues, and hair are a form of Earth. Saliva, urine, blood, and sweat are a form of Water. Fire inside of us creates hunger, thirst, and sleep. Air is responsible for all movement inside our body, including expansion, contraction, and suppression. Now, let's look at what happens when the balance of the five elements is disturbed.

Earth: If there is imbalance in the Earth element inside you, it can lead to overall weakness in the body, high cholesterol, weight loss or weight gain, bone or muscular pain, and issues.

Water: Imbalance in the element Water can cause cold and sinusitis, asthma, swelling of glands, blood thinning or clotting.

Air: Imbalance in the Air element may result in nervous disorders and depression, blood pressure issues, lung disorders, or muscle pains and spasms.

Fire: Imbalance in the element Fire can manifest itself as extreme variations in perceived temperature, coldness or fever, skin diseases, diabetes, or mental disorders.

Space: Imbalance in the Space element can become visible as thyroid disorders, throat and speech problems, epilepsy, or ear diseases, etc.

We breathe air and thus can blow it out of our mouths too. Our cells die and turn to dust, thus we produce Earth and when our bodies become infected with something foreign, we start to heat up thus we produce heat. We may think of these elements as individual and separate them, but ultimately, they are merely a form of the other. Similarly, within ourselves, we hold these elements which dictate our behaviour, mentality, and character.

For example, people with a dominant Earth element tend to be grounding as the element relates to Earth and is synonymous with terms such as foundation, roots, security, steadfastness, and the ability to create new things. People with this personality type are very stable, predictable, down to earth, disciplined, and love structure. For them, a structured life means a life guided by rules and discipline. They tend to like things scheduled and organised. For them, certain values never change, or they never compromise on them. This part of their personality is absolutely fixed and strong. People with an Earth personality are decisive and reliable, they are very committed however, sometimes this commitment even transforms into stubbornness. They are full of humility by nature. They are not only strong but also brutally honest and real. They tend to stay in the same job/profession as they don't feel comfortable with change. As small change as a change in neighbourhood or opinion affects them.

A person with an Earth element can be very depressed. They tend to do well in the field of mathematics, physics, statistics, chemistry, etc. Texting is also considered an earth quirk. A teacher with earth element tends to have a nice handwriting. A person with earth element has good communication skills, talks directly and gives no compliments. Their relationship focus is—I will show you by my actions, and I will do whatever you want.

There is an anger mindset in earth types, they react quickly; however, they tend to calm down quickly too. Sometimes they can be very blunt. People dominant in earth, know they are organised and know how to do what they need to do. They go from task to task with determination.

People with a dominant Water-type element have all the traits of a baby. Like a baby, they always want attention; they are emotional, and they are always pleasurable. Similar to how water naturally exists in three different stages and is very adaptable, people with a water dominant personality also have the ability to go with the flow and be comfortable with different situations. They also tend to enjoy new situations.

However, water element dominant people can be people pleasers, as they tend to have low self-esteem.

A lack of water indicates a lack of pleasure in life, similarly for water type people it indicates lack of willingness to live. These types of people don't have major motivations, as they are too busy catering to the needs of others. Water elements tend to attach to materialistic things and similarly when they feel uncomfortable with something, they take out that thing from their life.

People with a dominant Air type element have an easy-going personality opposite to the earth element. They tend to take things on a lighter note and rarely get into arguments. People with an airy personality have a broader perspective. Hence, they do not get consumed in detail. They are not as grounded and tend to look upwards. They are dreamers and visionaries who focus on imagination, exploration, adventure, and their goals.

If someone is narrow minded, inflexible, stubborn, and difficult to have a relationship with, Air dominant people can help them open up, and cultivate that element inside the other person too. Their interests lie in art and philosophy and are not very materialistic. They are a free spirit with no boundaries. They don't make any plans before starting any work. In other words, their work rarely has any structure. Air element is related with ability to speak and listen, communicate, and the ability to move and change. A person with significant air element is interested to learn about everyone and everything in this universe.

People with a dominant Fire-type element tend to show all the features of fire itself. They have a drive to do something significant. This drive might even turn into anger or resentment towards something or someone. Just like fire, sometimes they are hard to control when they're excited.

Fire illuminates and eliminates, its constructive and destructive, similarly a person with fire dominance inside can become a beacon of creation as well as destruction. As fire rises, it defies the gravity as it flickers, this personality type also has an idea of transcending, looking upward, looking for something which is more than oneself. They have a passion for reaching a higher cause. They allow themselves to dream and restlessly aspire to reach their goals.

On a spiritual level, these people tend to be deep thinkers and are always questioning who put us here, who we are, and they search for a purpose. They tend to have anxiety. They identify with the colour red, which signifies concentration, guidance, and focus.

The Five Senses

"Equipped with his five senses, man explores the universe around him and calls the adventure 'Science.'"

– Edwin Powell Hubble

Most of the gross objects carry all the five senses such as sight, sound, smell, touch, and taste. The senses are worthless if we can't experience the outward world. Sense of sight is relevant only if there is something to see. We as human beings are able to recognise the physical world around us through our five organs of perception. Without them, we would not be aware of the physical world. Those five senses are: hearing, touch, sight, taste, and smell. This is a commonly known fact; however, there are some things that are not so widely known. The five senses each are closely related to one of the five elements; space, air, fire, water, and earth.

Space and the Sense of Hearing

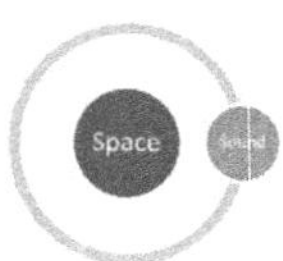

Sound is transmitted through space; thus, the element related to the hearing function is the organ of hearing, the ear, it expresses action through the organ of speech, which creates meaningful human sound.

Air and the sense of Touch

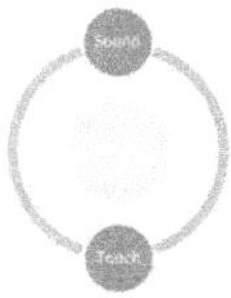

Skin is the sensory organ of touch. It is related to the Air element. Hand is the organ of action for the sense of touch. The hand is responsible for the actions of holding, giving as well as receiving.

Fire and the sense of Seeing

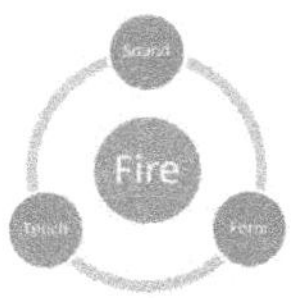

Fire gives birth to light, heat, and colour. It illuminates; thus, it is related to vision. The organ of sight are the eyes. The eye shows the way and give us direction and the feet take us forward; therefore, the feet are related to the action of seeing. Fire is energy, our eyes convert this energy to colour and light. Ultimately, fire not only shows us the way but also helps us move forward.

Water and the sense of Tasting

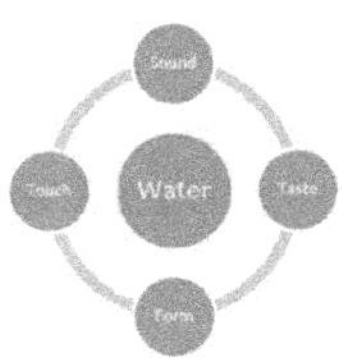

The sense of taste is related to Water; the tongue which is the organ of taste cannot taste if there is no water present. The tongue is also related to the action of the genitals in its function.

Earth and the sense of Smell

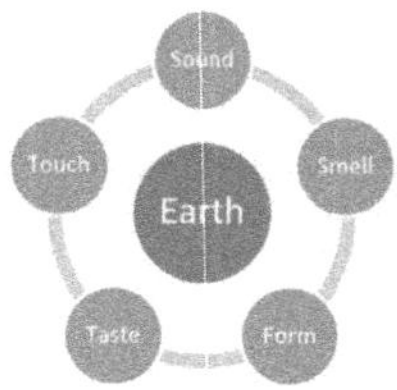

Our sense of smell is associated with element Earth and the sensory organ of smell is the nose. It is related in function to the action of the anus, excretion. A person who experiences bad breath or a duller sense of smell has constipation or an unclean colon; this fact demonstrates the relationship between the element and the sense. We might make the mistake of taking these essential elements for granted; however, it must not be forgotten that all life is derived from within these five basic elements. From the toy you used to play with when you were young to the devices you are holding now, the roots of all these creations are the five basic elements. Not only that, but these elements even have the power to manipulate the elements inside an individual's body; therefore, you should make sure to respect these elements and not abuse them in any way. Your disrespect can be as simple and tiny as glaring at a glass of water or stomping on the floor you walk on. It could be you abusing the fire inside you for the wrong reasons. For example, bullying the weak or getting into useless fights. If you abuse your elements, you'll pay a price, not just with your body but with your mind as well. So, live your life respecting everything and everyone around you. Use your fire for the better of yourself and others. If a universe is within you, make sure it's a peaceful one, a universe in order and not in chaos.

CHAPTER 6
THE MIND

Inside a human body, there exist two kinds of substances, tangible and intangible. Now, it's not difficult to identify the tangible parts in ourselves. It's the organs, skin, hands, and every part of us that exists in the physical realm. So, what are these intangible parts? You might have already guessed; it's our feelings, thoughts, imaginations, and emotions. All these intangible things exist in a space beyond physical, beyond reality. Evidently, they can't be touched, heard, or tasted because they aren't real, or it would be more proper to say that they are on a higher plane of existence than the physical and the metaphysical. A question that arises after these statements come into the light is that how are these things inside us. The answer to this question is that these things exist in our mind (Manas).

The mind is often confused with the brain as both being one and the same. However, this is far from the truth. Just as the difference between the tangible and intangible in the human body is quite evident, the difference between the brain and the mind can be explained using the same terms.

The brain is the tangible organ inside our body. Its functions are merely logical reasoning and controlling basic functions of the human body. The brain is devoid of emotions or feelings and is purely physical in its state. The mind, on the other hand, is intangible. It's a space that can be filled with whatever a person wishes. The mind is through which a person feels emotions, thinks without any limitations, and creates their own rules. It's a space where anything is possible. One can imagine themselves to be the king of that space, make their own rules, and create their wildest fantasies. However, there is a side effect. This mind is what creates our reality in the physical world as well. Our thoughts, feelings, and ambitions all affect the way in which we interact with the real world. Our fantasies and thoughts dictate our lives. The Buddha states:

"What you think you become."

This statement correctly describes the effects our mind has on our real life.

It is said that we live in a world of thought, as our thoughts create our experiences and in turn, we experience what we think. The only variable is the quality of your thoughts as they translate to the quality of your life. The mind has the ability to create and alter our reality. English philosopher named James Allen wrote:

"As a man thinks, so he is; as he continues to think, so he remains."

Most people, when unhappy, seek to create change in their lives; however, they make the grave mistake of thinking that change begins from the outside. To live a happy life, people transform their environment, believing that doing so will create the change they desire. They buy material objects, bigger, better, more efficient objects to boost their happiness. Some choose to leave their homeland and go about traveling the world, believing they can escape their problems by doing so. Whereas, some go as far as consuming harmful substances to numb their pain. However, nothing changes for such people who believe that their happiness depends on external factors, and they helplessly fall back down into their pit of unhappiness and misery.

There's no doubt that external factors and environment plays a role in changing an individual's circumstances, but it doesn't address the root of the problem. The reason you feel the way you do is due to "your mind" or simply saying, what manifests in your mind, your thoughts.

"If you get the inside right, the outside will fall into place."

– Eckhart Tolle

To change your outside (your circumstances), you must first change the inside. Changing the direction of your thoughts will directly influence how you feel.

How you feel will influence how your body reacts. Your reactions directly influence your behaviour, which ultimately dictates who you are and how you experience life. Our thoughts, which are the manifestation of the mind by themselves, are powerless. However, when you actively pursue those thoughts and invest your time and attention thinking about them, they will start to transcend to your reality. These thoughts trigger certain emotions, which can be easily transferred to the physical world through our facial expressions, and ultimately, these emotions start influencing our actions.

If we take the example of a person who usually manifests thoughts of depression, worries, and thinks about being a failure, all these thoughts will influence how he acts. He may start showing signs of depression such as low self-confidence, slumped shoulders, and low energy. On the other hand, if a person indulges himself with positive and empowering thoughts, it would trigger a more positive emotional state which would reflect in his body. He would have a confident stance and an energetic composure.

The mind and the body are connected in more ways than just physical. They are allies, and one's illness directly affects the other. An example of this connection is how your body responds to mental stress. Stress over family, finances, job, etc., causes muscles in our body to tense. We experience headaches, stomach problems, and constant stress, which can also lead to serious health issues such as high blood pressure. Similarly, when your body is ill, your mind also becomes infected; for example, bodily health complications such as cancer, disability, or heart problems can lead you to depression, anxiety, and other serious mental health issues.

Harness the power of the mind to improve your emotional health and to live a balanced life. Let's look at a few ways you can gain control over your emotions.

1. **Express your emotions**: keeping feelings of stress and sadness inside can cause significant health issues. A proper and effective solution to this problem is to converse with a loved one about your problems. Sharing your pain and sadness will lighten the heavy load inside you, and a loved one might also advise and help you deal with your problems.
2. **Balance your mind**: obsessing over the negative aspects of your life will only lead you to the path of constant worry and misery. So, focus on the good your life has to offer. Practise mindfulness and think about everything you are grateful for in your life. Let go of what causes stress and appreciate the things that make you feel peaceful and content.
3. **Calm your mind and body**: our body is merely a vessel for our soul, and our soul is made of pure elemental energy, therefore, one must consume a diet comprised of whole foods and limit their consumption of a heavily processed diet. Similarly, you can practise various relaxation techniques such as meditation, yoga, listening to music, or painting to calm your mind. Anything

> that provides peace to your mind and brings balance to your life.

In Sanskrit Mind is also known as "Manas." The Manas separates human beings from animals. Even though animals possess a brain, they lack the intellect to utilise the past impressions of their experiences. As discussed earlier, the brain and mind are poles apart. The brain is the physical organ in your body, while mind is something which is neither visible nor audible, it can only be experienced. It's the part of the body where thought takes place. The Manas is never silent. You might have noticed chatter in your mind, a continuous chain of thought, one after the other, this constant stream of thoughts is the result of our mind. Our mind always keeps talking about our mistakes, our mischief, our guilt, self-criticism, rejection, jealousy, loneliness, insult, failure in the past and apprehension, fear, insecurity, anxiety, worry, concern and nervousness pertaining to the future. It is never quiet. Sometimes these constant and haphazard thoughts overpower a person, creating unhealthy and abnormal habits within them; an example of this is the people who are seen talking to themselves.

There's also a medical condition associated with this chatter of the mind called "Logorrhoea." In this condition, a person is forced to utter every random thought that occurs in his mind. "Schizophrenia" is another mental condition with similar symptoms, but it is far worse than Logorrhoea.

It is commonly said that a healthy mind resides in a healthy body. Most of our bad habits and issues start from our mind; it compels us to do bad things and makes it extremely difficult to renounce any bad habits. As a human, we don't always act on every impulse. That's where our brain comes in and helps us reason with our mind. Similarly, all spiritual leaders, writers, engineers, and doctors are also the product of the human mind. In short, only with the proper coordination of the brain and mind, can we live a life that is balanced and fulfilling.

We discussed earlier that the mind doesn't exist on the physical plane of existence, so if it's not in the real world then how was it formed, how does it function, how to come over its perpetual chatter and above all how to train our mind to become more productive. Let's dive in deeper into the Manas and talk about the greatest friend of mankind as well as the greatest foe called "The Mind."

Formation of the Mind

Science has given the world millions of inventions and breakthroughs, but there is still one thing science can't find the answer to "How is life created." Life is created without consulting us. It's an unknown process about which we know nothing. After the biological process of conception, a foetus starts forming in a mother's womb, slowly and steadily it gains organs, skin, and senses, but how does it come to life in the first place? Or in simpler terms, how does it gain a "soul?" How and when does the soul become part of the foetus? Where does this soul come from? Countless questions arise.

It is said that everything in this universe has a background history. Similarly, when life becomes part of the foetus, it also comes with a history. The foetus has also gone through various emotions of the mother who is carrying it. It feels all the good as well as bad emotions of the mother, and through her, experiences the outside world. In the east, there is an important terminology for this called "Garbh-Sanskara." This means, the impression that a baby receives of the outside world when it is still in the mother's womb.

Apart from the past life history and Garbh-Sanskara, the actual process of formation of the mind starts once the baby is born. When the baby opens his eyes for the first time and utters its first cry, the real experiences start. It starts feeling the atmosphere, the touch of others, and as the number of days and weeks pass by, it starts learning. The first action the baby performs is flipping on its side, then it starts crawling, learns how to sit and stand. Later, it takes the first step and starts walking confidently. It also starts babbling a few sounds and later speaks a whole sentence clearly. In the process of learning, it comes across many failures. It falls down many times, hurts itself, and repeats the same action again and again to learn a new skill. It learns by trial and error and changes its actions accordingly. These early experiences become the basis of all learning. The baby learns new things by coming into contact with the outside world and its various elements. All these experiences combine to create a consciousness, a mind. Let's look at a few factors which matter the most in the formation of a mind.

The Family:

> *"Being a family means you are a part of something very wonderful. It means you will love and be loved for the rest of your life."*
>
> – Lisa Weed

According to modern sociology, the family is the primary institute of socialisation for an individual because the earliest years of one's life are spent surrounded by their family. From the moment of birth, the first interaction of the outside world a baby has is with the family in which it is born. Its mother is the first person it gets in touch with. It learns the beliefs, cultures, traditions, and traits of its mother and father and of his family. It plays, fights, and interacts with its siblings and shares all its early experiences with them. The baby learns to laugh as well as cry with its family and thus develops a strong bond with its family. This early bond formed with the family forms the basis of its existence as they provide a feeling of home, security, and comfort, even if the family fails to provide the baby with things of great value, it still gets a feeling of peace among them.

Education System:

> *"Education is simply the soul of a society as it passes from one generation to another."*
>
> – G.K. Chesterton

After family, the second institute of socialisation is the school where a child meets peers of similar age. These interactions breed many wonderful concepts such as friendliness, gratitude, and empathy. Additionally, schools also teach a child basic mannerism such as how to speak, eat, and play properly and build a conscience which helps a child differentiate right from wrong. The education system plays a vital role in moulding our mind as schools are a place of discovering new things and introduce us to foreign concepts. All this knowledge breeds curiosity which leads to creativity and ultimately exploration.

Religious beliefs:

Religion is an important aspect of an individual's life. Our religion and beliefs are a basic component of our surroundings and society. Our religion also helps us reinforce certain beliefs in our mind. Due to their early influence, these belief systems take up a permanent spot in our minds and a major part of our life is spent on defending our belief systems. Sometimes, these beliefs are so strong that people die for their sake. These beliefs can relate to anything—they may be related to our religion, our cast and creed, colour of the skin, language or practically anything else. These belief systems are so foundational in some people that they are ready to go as far as to kill others for the sake of protecting their beliefs.

Economic Status:

An individual's financial situation also has a huge impact on their mind. There's no doubt that our society has disparity. It is said that the top 20% of the people possess more than 80% of the wealth in the world. The world of those who live in slums and struggle to make ends meet and those who are wealthy and affluent are completely different. Similarly, their thought processes and mindsets are also completely different. Both have lived a different life and were brought up differently which is why they think and behave differently.

Parts of the Mind

The mind is defined by four parts: memory, intellect, ego, and consciousness. Many people think that memory is stored in the brain; however, that is not true, and a simple example that proves this statement wrong is the concept of muscle memory. Memory is the experience from the past so not only our brain but every cell inside our body has its own memory.

There are several types of memory. Some of them are as follows:

- Evolutionary memory – The process of evolution which started billions of years ago. We are a part of that process, and our DNA is the proof of that. We still have inside of us the remnant of the first cell created.

- Genetic memory – Genetic memory is the memory we inherit from our forefathers and ancestors. From our race, height, and weight to even the quality of health we will have, all is inherited from our parents. An example of this is the genetic diseases that one can get from their parents, such as Huntington's disease.
- Karmic memory– It is said that Karma creates memories and desires, and these desires and memories then determine how you live. The subtle energy created by your actions is stored inside you, within your memories and desires, and these memories can be activated through stimulus or by themselves sometimes in the future. There have been many instances in the world when people suddenly develop fear or phobia. We normally develop fear from an object, or phobia from specific situations we may have faced in the past. However, if the phobia comes out of nowhere, it is said to be Karmic baggage. People who work with psychological healing such as Hypnotherapists, work on the Karmic baggage of a person. This baggage can be from this life or the life of their ancestors (or in some culture from their past lives).
- Sensory memory – How we interact with the external world is the result of our senses. Our senses give us the ability to interact and react to the things happening around us, and because of this, we can learn to avoid tasting and smelling anything, which is not pleasant to our senses.

- Inarticulate and Articulate memories – The mind is home to millions of thoughts, each with a particular information and our unconscious mind constantly interacts with them. These packets of random information can be grouped to be called inarticulate memory whereas our conscious interaction with those thoughts and information we store within ourselves are an example of articulate memories.

During your life, you make hundreds of memories, some are good and some are bad. This contradiction hinders the judgements you make towards a certain event or person. If you prioritise the negative memories, it will feel like you haven't done anything worthwhile in your life. Because your mind is confused, it interprets your life as joyless. It is important to understand what you have been given, as we know our body is a very sophisticated machine. If any confusion occurs within our cells, your life will feel empty. Therefore, it is imperative to keep our memories in sync, and only then, will our lives be balanced. Similarly, it is the duty of an individual to feed their mind with knowledge, only then the intellect will flourish. As it is rightly said by Alan Moore:

"Don't leave home without your sword - your intellect."

Ego and consciousness are other essential parts of your mind. Ego is a person's self-esteem; it's the importance one gives to his own self. On the other hand, consciousness, at its simplest, is sentience or awareness of one's internal and external existence. It's the knowledge of being a conscious, existing entity that is part of a grand scheme of events much larger than himself, and at the same time knowing that you have an important role to play in this scheme. All these aspects combine to create the "Manas."

Brain Waves:

The brain is a miraculous instrument. It is an interface to our mind. The brain has a centre called the "Cerebrum", which is responsible for thinking. As thoughts starts in the mind, they are illuminated by small electric pulses. As the number of thoughts increases, the mind's electrical pulses also increase. This produces brain waves.

Let's take a look at the four different types of waves:

- <u>Gamma Wave (Kshipta manas)</u> – When the brain is in the Gama state, it's in a state of wakefulness and can quickly shift its focus from one object or subject to another. Gamma brain waves are the fastest waves produced inside your brain. When your brain is producing gamma waves, you have achieved peak concentration. These waves help you process information and during this state, your brain is very actively engaged in solving a problem. Meditation and focused breathing are two of the best ways you can increase the gamma waves inside your brain.

- Beta Waves (Vikshipt Manas) – In this state, the mind processes a wide range of information without focusing on one object. These are the brain waves that dominate your brain when you're awake, alert, and engaged. It's a wave one step below from gamma. During this state, you are casually thinking about many things at once.
- Alpha Waves (Mudha) - A state when the mind is dull and not seeking new knowledge. Alpha waves fit somewhere between theta and beta waves. During this state, your mind is relaxed and not thinking about any particular subject. These waves occur when you're probably feeling relatively calm and relaxed. If you're actively able to produce alpha brain waves, you'll be able to consciously tap into a state that can help you get some rest and relaxation.
- Theta Waves (Ekagrata) - A state when the mind is focused on one subject and remains focused on it without getting distracted. Theta brain waves occur during sleep or when dreaming; however, these waves do not occur during the deepest phase of your sleep. They are dominant in the brain in a state of half wakefulness or just before waking. These brain waves can also occur when you are awake but in a deeply relaxed state. Some may describe that state as "autopilot." High levels of theta waves while you're awake can make you feel lazy or sluggish.
- Delta Waves (Nirudhha) – This state is when the mind is in complete control of an individual,

and spiritual elevation is achieved. These waves reside all the way at the bottom of the wave spectrum, below theta waves. During the production of delta waves, your brain is in a deep state of rest and sleep. These waves keep the overall brain activity to a minimum and allow restorative processes to take place throughout the body.

Nature of the Mind

Picture a Rubik's cube continuously solving and unsolving itself; that is what the mind is like. It's a constant stream of millions of thought patterns folding and unfolding onto each other. Dr Joe Dispenza claims that by thinking positively, we can make our bodies and minds healthier. The mind is conscious of everything whether interior or exterior; however, most of us have conditioned our minds to think negatively. Instead of being present in a situation and consciously embracing the positive, most people choose to think about the regrets of the past or worry over the future. This must be avoided and only positive must be embraced.

The No Mind Situation

This might sound strange, but I'm sure many of you must be aware of and might even have experienced the "No mind situation." In fact, we experience it every day. Every day, when we are in a state of rest and sleep, we are free from all kinds of worldly distress and sorrow.

The no mind situation is a state when the experiences of our mind don't bother us; however, these experiences come back to us when we wake.

Achieving the no mind stage in the state of wakefulness is a tough deed, but it's not impossible to accomplish. The no mind state allows you to think and experience beyond the plane of reality. It allows you to see the things that are important and those that are irrelevant. The experiences of the physical world, the day to-day life of an individual, the work they do, the family they take care of, and every other aspect of their life is a binding aspect. These factors make it hard for individuals to reach the no mind state. However, if you abandon the thought that this world you're living in is everything and realise that there is a higher plane of existence where you're meant to be; only then you will be able to achieve the no mind state while you're awake.

Many people, especially youngsters, believe that this state is achievable through psychedelics substances. They make a habit of consuming these harmful substances to put themselves in a state of relaxation. However, this counterfeit state they put themselves in is not a no mind state, as a matter of fact this is just a state like sleep and as is the fact that one cannot stay asleep forever.

Instead, we should practise every day to reach a state where our bodies can sustain these changes. Slowly and steadily, we can learn to create a situation where we can train ourselves to signal our mind to switch off and remain at peace within itself. We should train ourselves to make this happen at any time and any place. It should be entirely up to us as to when we want help from the experiences that we have attained from our mind and when the past experiences are unneeded.

A couple of years back, I met a student of mine. He asked me the solution for a situation he used to face every day while trying to study. Upon my persistent enquiry, he revealed that his mind wanders and he starts thinking about pornographic movies whenever he tries to concentrate and focus on his studies which ultimately leads to him completely forgetting his studies and his hand running down his pants. Similarly, another true story is about a person who would overeat. He felt compelled to eat before starting any kind of work and several times in between, for no reason. These situations are very difficult to overcome when we have spoiltour mind and body by continuous self-gratification. Gradually, these acts turn into a habit which only leads to us looking for a more gratifying pleasure, and the worst part is that even though we realise that our habits are not doing us any good, we still find it hard to overcome them.

It is said that you can create a new habit if you do something continuously for 21 days. Doing this requires sheer determination and discipline, and the no mind situation is great to overcome any unhealthy habit. The first and foremost thing to do is to still your mind and face your own self as an outside entity. Judge yourself as someone who is looking at you as an outsider. This is where cosmic intelligence will also play a huge part; when you look at yourself as the universe looks at you, it becomes easier to identify your flaws and weaknesses. Use your wisdom and look for the catalyst that forces you to act out your bad habit. Once you have identified that catalyst in your mind and understood your own thought patterns, you must distance yourself from it and find a meaningful task to replace it with. For example, if you feel compelled to eat again and again, try reducing the snacks you have in your house. Once you limit the resources, you'll have no choice but to distract yourself, and if this is done continuously, you'll be able to stop acting out a certain habit.

The mind is a complex structure; it is constantly changing and extremely flexible. As humans, we have always been told to use our brain to solve the simplest as well as the most sophisticated of problems; however, it is not just our brain that untangles the mysteries of life but also our mind. The mind projects hundreds of possibilities before us even before we start thinking about a situation consciously. Therefore, it is imperative to foster a healthy mind to gain control over your body and its habits.

CHAPTER 7
THE ENERGY REALM

We have discussed on multiple occasions that the body is a container, a vessel for the soul. However, it's not just any vessel, so why should it be given any less importance? Just as understanding our mind is vital for our existence, similar is the case with the body. Nowadays, it has become common for people to have ill health. Everyone is facing issues of one kind or another. There are more hospitals than before, more doctors, better living situations, yet we have more people facing sickness and ill health. Ever wondered why?

People have now shifted their focus more and more towards science. They get regular health checks, take medications yet struggle to exist. It's precisely their increased belief in science and medicine that leads them to this path of unhealthy habits. People think it's okay to eat a highly processed, full of grease meal because they can take a pill later to digest quickly. They choose to take calcium supplements instead of taking it naturally through milk or yogurt. They consume unhealthy amounts of caffeine and other carbonated drinks to increase their productivity instead of focusing on a more regular schedule and eating whole foods. Basic practises of following a regular sleep schedule, eating right, and getting the right amount of exercise are probably some of the easiest and simplest practises one can follow, which will allow the body to flourish and become more active. These practises will not only regulate your physical health but also affect your spiritual and mental health. However, many people face the challenge of not being able to work through their physical, mental, and spiritual concerns; they are confused and don't know where and how to begin. Their mind and body resist change, becoming rigid and unable to move forward in their lives. Let's take a look to see why some people must face this problem.

Chakras

We discussed earlier that a source is needed to keep the body alive. This energy source comes from "The Energy Realm," and it travels in our body in a state similar to electric signals. Like an electrical interface, these channels inside our body also form junctions. When the channels meet at these junction points, a vibration is created, and a ripple is emitted. These ripples are circular and are called "Chakras."

These chakras are what keep our bodies alive and well. There are 114 such junction points in the human body. However, these points are guided by the seven most essential junction points located along the spine. These seven junction points, also known as chakras, are directly related to our seven endocrine glands responsible for essential functions in our body. All these endocrine glands secrete specific hormones and are responsible for a specific function of our existence. These chakras are thought to be spinning disks of energy that should stay "open" and aligned, as they correspond to different organs, nerves, and areas of our energetic body that affect our emotions as well as physical well-being. Each of these seven main chakras have a corresponding number, name, and colour, and are located in a specific area of the spine from the crown of the head to the root of the spine. In addition, each of these seven chakras has a specific health and wellness focus.

The colours of chakras vary from red to violet, and these colours correspond pretty accurately with the cultural and societal meanings given to them. For example, red is used to imply a sense of danger or threat. Similarly, our existence, the body is related to red, which is fragile and danger to it can cause the end of life. Hence the red colour is related to our life.

There are seven different names of the chakras as we go from the tip of our backbone to the top of our brain. These points are as follows:

These chakras are like a pool of energy, and any disruption in them corresponds to a particular wellness symptom. Physical as well as emotional symptoms, can manifest depending upon which chakra is out of balance. The symptoms can range between fatigue, anxiety, and unwillingness to do work. Each chakra is also connected to a particular element and deals with a specific plain of our existence. For example, some chakras focus on the physical body, whereas some focus on the spiritual body. These chakras represent a set of emotions that can drastically impact an individual's health and overall success in life. Therefore, working with our chakras, understanding their particular impacts, and keeping them flowing has significant physical, emotional, psychological, and spiritual benefits.

When we talk about chakras, there is another crucial concept that we must understand about the human body. Besides the seven major energy pools known as chakras, there are three main "Nadis" in the human body. The root word for Nadi is Nada which is the Sanskrit word for "sound", and sound is created from vibrations. Originally, there were 72000 Nadis in the body. These 72000 Nadis are vibration channels spread throughout your body. When these channels intersect, they form energy points, which we all know as chakras. Just like chakras, these Nadis are not physical and cannot be measured; however, they can be perceived at psychic levels as distinct channels of light, colour, and sound. The three main Nadi systems in the body are Ida, Pingla, and Shushumna. Ida runs along the left side of your body, Pingla runs along the right, and Shushumna runs along the centre. All three of these Nadis are said to have distinct characteristics.

Ida is feminine in nature and associated with creativity. This Nadi is also associated with the moon as it's said to have a moon-like calming and cooling effect on the body. Pingla, on the other hand, is masculine and analytical in nature. Pingla means "orange" in the Sanskrit language. It is associated with the sun and solar energy, and it provides life energy and heat energy to the body. These Nadis are often referred to as the two hemispheres of the brain. Pingla corresponds to the left hemisphere and is seen as having extroverted tendencies, whereas Ida is associated with the right hemisphere and is seen dominating the introverted tendencies of a person. So, a person who is right-brain dominant will be creative and a left-brain dominant person will be analytical.

Due to its analytic nature, Ida is said to control mental processes, and Pingla is said to control the vital processes of the human body. Shushumna is said to connect the base chakra to the crown chakra. It has significant importance in yogic and tantric rituals as it's the channel along which all seven chakras reside.

Naturally, all three of these Nadi systems are unblocked, but due to many reasons such as worldly entanglements, financial, emotional, or mental stress, they get blocked. However, there are many effective processes that can help reactivate them, such as breathing techniques, yoga, and the best among all, meditation. The Nadi system is the foundational energy system in the human body. Chakras are also a by-product of this basic energy system and just like the three Nadis, each of the seven chakras has a distinct set of characteristics and associates with a particular set of physical and mental symptoms.

Root Chakra

The root chakra is based in the root of the spine and is masculine in nature, which means it is an energy generator for the outside world and your body. It is affiliated with the red colour, and its element is Earth. Your root chakra establishes your physical presence as it is referred to as being foundational and grounding. Through your root chakra the Earth's energy can communicate with our body. There is also a subsidiary chakra in the heels of our body connected with our root chakra. These subsidiary chakras work and are only helpful if there is a strong root chakra.

Anger is an emotion associated with the root chakra. If you are suppressing your anger, it means you are suppressing the gift of the root chakra. Suppression of one's emotions directly relates to the agreeableness of a person. A person who is too agreeable and struggles to say "No" is a person who doesn't want to create a critical situation or doesn't want anyone to be angry with them. If you don't know how to say "No," your root chakra is not balanced, and you need to work on it. Root chakra reminds you that you are here for yourself and not anyone else.

There are a few questions you can ask yourself to find out if your root chakra is weak or strong:

1. Do you have low energy in the morning?
2. Do you feel insecure about your body and looks?

If yes, then you have a weak root chakra. When your root chakra is weak, you feel as if your legs are weak and shaky. The feeling that you are unsafe always looms over you. With a weak root chakra, people constantly tend to feel like a victim. They project all their energy away and towards the outside world as they don't feel like facing the world. Procrastination and the inability to take action are also signs of a weak root chakra.

On the other hand, if you have a strong root chakra, you'll feel more safe, relaxed, strong, and grounded. The Root chakra is also associated with the adrenaline gland, which initiates the fight or flight response. The root chakra is all about empowering oneself. It reinforces the idea that you are the creator of your life, and only you can enhance your reality.

Sacral Chakra

Sacral Chakra is positioned just above your root chakra. It governs your emotions and sexuality. The endocrine gland associated with the sacral chakra is the testes/ ovaries. The colour associated with the sacral chakra is orange, the colour of life, vibrancy, and enjoyment. It's a feminine chakra; it receives energy and is sensitive to energy. Its associated element is water. A person who has a balanced sacral chakra is a pleasurable person to be around. Whatever emotions they firmly adhere to, the sacral chakra will enhance that emotion. What is the emotion you are most familiar with? That is the prime emotion you have related to the sacral chakra. People with a strong sacral chakra are sitting on a throne of emotions. They are compassionate and empathetic. Sacral chakra teaches us the dynamics of love and hate. Like waves, the emotions in such a person sometimes go high and sometimes low. Sacral chakra magnifies the joy you see in the world; it magnifies opportunities by seeing them everywhere. A strong sacral chakra allows you to feel abundance in the world.

On the other hand, a person with a weak sacral chakra has difficulty having fun and enjoying things. The sacral chakra, the chakra of emotions, is spoilt easily if not taken care of properly. For the people who have a powerful sacral chakra, life is difficult as they are too empathetic; they feel the emotions of others and make them their own. The sacral chakra dictates our likes, dislikes, things that we love, and hate everything. People are sometimes overwhelmed by these emotions, so how should we deal with such a situation? You have to ground yourself. Go back to the strengths of your root chakra. Be mindful and pay attention to your emotions. Identify what you are feeling and separate yourself from unfamiliar emotions. As soon as you realise that what you are carrying inside are someone else's emotions, you will be able to free yourself from those emotions.

Sacral chakra works like a magnet. By programming your sacral chakra, you can attract your desires. You are asking the universe to give you your desires and needs. All you need to do is plant the seed of the emotion you want to experience. Sacral chakra helps you intensify that emotion and attract it from the universe.

Solar Chakra

Solar Chakra, also called *Manipuraka,* is the seat of the soul. It's the seat of confidence and willpower. It's a masculine chakra in nature and associated with the colour yellow, located in the stomach, also known as the house of your soul, the centre of you. It is associated with the element of Fire. The solar chakra enhances your confidence and willpower. People with a strong solar chakra are doers and leaders in nature.

People who gain control of the solar chakra focus on winning and tend to be business-minded. If you have a strong solar chakra, you have the will to do something exceptional. You have a good attitude towards winning and achievement, and the ability to believe in yourself.

People with high solar chakra have a seed of healthy ego, which provides them with confidence and a sense of individualism; however, developing that healthy ego and balancing it depends on the person.

There is a fire in people with a strong solar chakra. However, that fire is finite. If you spend your willpower doing something insignificant, such as watching TV or browsing the internet for no reason, it will lessen your productivity. You will need to recharge your willpower at the end of the day when it is depleted. You can recharge it by sleeping, meditation, breathing, and prioritising your goals.

Many people with a strong solar chakra face a dilemma. "Do you want to be yourself or copy others?" The third chakra sets an individual apart from others and makes them unique. One has to have the courage to accept that they are different. Your uniqueness will set you apart from the herd. The challenge is that here, you empower yourself. You live your own path and follow it alone. Sometimes that is painful and challenging.

Heart Chakra

Heart Chakra, also known as *Anahata,* is the link between this physical life and the cosmos. It is the place of interconnectedness, oneness with God, cosmos, and love that connects us all.

This is a feminine chakra in nature situated in the centre of the chest, and the endocrine gland associated with this is the heart (Thymus). The heart chakra is where healing takes place. Imagine the hands of a healer, someone giving generously; those are the symbolisms associated with the Heart chakra. The colour associated with the heart chakra is green, and the element is Air.

This chakra is all about love and compassion. People with a strong heart chakra see love in everything. They feel like they are connected with everyone. They also start to feel a connection with God. People with a strong heart chakra get teary-eyed very quickly. They get emotional over things, sometimes they feel intense sadness and sometimes intense happiness.

The key to unlocking the heart is forgiveness. It is hard to forgive someone, especially when they have done something wrong to you. We can hold people accountable for what they have done. But understand that everyone on this planet is on a learning journey. Once you open your heart chakra, you can connect with yourself and others. You can feel and empathise; you can respond to someone distressed or in pain. A happy heart creates more happy hearts.

People with a weak heart chakra feel as if the world is unlovable. They can't love someone or something because something terrible happened to them. Someone broke their heart or didn't return their compassion. Therefore, it is also harmful to give too much to the world. There is a fine line between helping someone and letting them exploit you.

To heal your heart and strengthen your chakra, you should practise charity. Acts of kindness will show you how beautiful the world is as you learn about other compassionate people. Practise forgiveness and letting things go. People who have done something terrible did not do those things to you but themselves, so why must you bear the burden of hatred.

Throat Chakra

This Chakra is also known as *Vishudhi*, meaning filter. It is the home of expression and governs our relationship with the outside world. People who have mastered the art of expression become authors, musicians, and successful public speakers. It is located in your throat, above your heart. The throat chakra is masculine in nature. It projects energy to the outside world and is related to the endocrine gland called the thyroid. The thyroid is responsible for the metabolism in your body. It is like the control centre of the body and manages how you use your energy. The element it is related to is the Sky (Ether), and it's associated with the colour blue. Through words you can change the feelings in the body of other people and your own. Words are very powerful to incite the feelings of the lower four chakras.

The throat chakra is essential for the personal and professional growth. Words create your reality. The power of affirmation is one of the ways to cast a great spell of reassurance on yourself. Similarly, you can also cast your influence onto others.

Throat chakra deals with truth. So, when you lie, who are you lying to? Others or yourself? When we communicate, we first talk to ourselves, then to others. If you feel like lying, it shows that your throat chakra is closed. The feelings of insecurity while speaking or the urge to hide the truth is associated with a weak throat chakra. However, when this chakra is blown open, you feel confident with your words and don't feel like hiding the truth.

Third Eye Chakra

In Sanskrit it is known as *Agyaan*, meaning command centre. The domain of the mind. The third eye chakra is associated with the colour indigo and governs imagination and intuition. It is the seat of higher perception, vision, and intuition. While throat chakra speaks the truth, it's the job of the third eye chakra to uncover the truth. Learning and obtaining knowledge are related to the third eye chakra.

The third eye chakra is related to the pituitary gland, a small, bean-shaped gland situated at the base of your brain, somewhat behind your nose and between your ears. Despite its small size, the gland influences nearly every part of your body, and the hormones it produces help regulate essential functions, such as growth, blood pressure, and reproduction.

The third eye helps you make decisions. This chakra is closed when you satisfy your mind with information and opens again when you actively seek something new.

The third eye chakra is where your thoughts, beliefs, and decisions take shape. With the help of the third eye chakra, you can construct and deconstruct your reality. If something is not the way you want it to be, you can change the belief and re-write a new belief system. Your beliefs and your mind will shape your reality. Just as we eat food to nourish our body, we seek an information diet for our mind.

Resistance to new information, not changing your beliefs, or updating them based on new facts is a sign of a closed third eye chakra. Inflexibility and having a hard time understanding a situation also shows a weak third eye.

On the other hand, looking for new information and learning is a sign of a strong third eye chakra. Sometimes this results in overthinking and paranoia; however, meditation is a great way to clear the mind and remove all information from your mind that is not required. The third eye chakra is the space to perceive what is going on within you. Once you can actively open your third eye chakra, the world will appear clearer and fuller.

Crown Chakra

Crown Chakra represents openness to divine inspiration and the complete surrender to higher intelligence. This is known as *Sahasrar* (thousand petaled), opening thousand aspects of our existence. Your willingness to be a part of a higher ego.

The crown chakra is located at the top of your head, pointing and downloading information, also known as the cosmic antenna. Violet in colour, it deals with the mysterious sublime realms of reality—worlds of angels and demons. It is also very closely associated with the Pineal gland, which produces melatonin, a serotonin derived hormone that modulates sleep patterns.

The crown chakra is about learning how to surrender. While the third chakra is about confidence, willpower, and control, the crown chakra is about surrender, and you surrender when you think there is something more potent than you; you surrender, bow down, and leave yourself in the hands of that supremely potent being.

Once you realise that you have done enough and surrender everything to become more efficient, this concept is usually beyond a rational mind. It does not fall in the scope of logic, mind, and reasoning.

I have realised it myself so many times; when you ask from the cosmos, you are reaffirmed and realise that it has already happened to you. You need to sit back and wait for your dream to materialises. Then someone or something will give you a sign, a symbol that is so subtle that you need to realise and pay attention, and you will understand what this cosmos wants from you. Divine guidance might show up in the form of a family member, friend, enemy, colour, or anything you come across. It may come in the dead of night.

For most people, this chakra is the hardest to master as it asks you to surrender yourself completely; however, those who can open it can receive guidance from the cosmos. Out of nowhere, they find themselves being in the right place at the right time, and good things start happening to them.

The body is a sea of energy, and many different types of flow exist in a single body. For example, there may be days when you feel extra confident or extra wise. Similarly, there may come days when you feel extra gloomy and irritated. Realise that all these things happen due to an imbalance in your energies. Once you understand this system, you can use it to your advantage.

CHAPTER 8
THE MOMENT

An individual's daily life is filled with many different problems and pleasures. To make their lives worthwhile, people work day and night, chase their dreams and desires, and try to recreate their fantasies. People go to all lengths to live a fulfilled life, yet one must be empty to be full. They are told that to realise fullness, one must experience an empty and calm mind. They are told to experience the "no-mind."

> *"Meditation is a state of no-mind! You cannot find meditation through the mind...because the mind will perpetuate itself! You can find meditation only by putting the mind aside, by being cool, indifferent, unidentified with the mind."*
>
> – Rajneesh

No Mind and The Dilemma of Being Present

The No-Mind is a state of pure consciousness. It is a state where one doesn't experience any thoughts, beliefs, ideas, emotions, or connections—just plain emptiness. People are often confused when it comes to understanding the no-mind state. However, there is no way this state of consciousness can be explained through simple words. The no-mind doesn't have a thorough definition or explanation; instead, it's a relative experience of bliss and purity. One way to make the term clearer for people is to ask them to define the mind. What is the mind? It's a place of thoughts, ideas, and imagination. So, what is no mind? Simple, it's the exact opposite of mind; no thoughts, ideas, or imagination.

It is a known fact that thinking is the fundamental nature of the mind, so when no thinking occurs, that is the state of no-mind. Try to think of a time when you were so engrossed in an activity that all of your concentration was focused on one thing; try to remember if you were thinking about anything during that particular activity. For example, when you were watching a movie, and all your attention was focused on it. That is a state when you weren't thinking about anything other than the movie. No problems existed for you, no distractions, just you and your activity of interest. Has it ever happened to you that you are deeply invested in a book, and yet suddenly you realise that you weren't able to fully comprehend the paragraph you just finished reading, so you go back and reread it? In this scenario, in the middle of reading the book, your concentration shifted, and you started thinking about random things, causing you to lose focus and a sense of continuity in the story you were just reading. The state of mind distracted you. You suddenly remember that you have assignments due or you have to do chores or something else. Whereas, in the no-mind state, there is no thinking, no mind. There is only sheer focus and concentration.

> *"Presence of mind is really a state of no-mind. You can call it Mindfulness, Awareness, or you can call it a state of No-Mind."*
>
> – Osho

It is human nature to be restless and to think about problems or solutions of the past or future. So, whenever the mind is not restless, there is no mind. We say no mind because the mind cannot be restless, just like it's in the nature of a snake to bite, the mind's nature is to think; it cannot stop thinking, and there is no stop button for the mind. So, in the state of no-mind, the mind is simply not present. If it were, it wouldn't be a state of no mind. Now, many of you might be thinking about how the mind can disappear; it's an essential part of us. That is not true; remember, the mind and the brain are different. I'm not saying the brain disappears; the brain is physical and cannot phase away. The mind, on the other hand, is not a physical entity. That is why it is possible for there to be a state of no mind.

In this state of no-mind, you can realise that nothing separates you from anyone or anything. The mind creates the illusion of difference and separation. The mind is either occupied with the thoughts of the past or the future, which robs us of the opportunity to be in the present. Thinking about past mistakes only pulls us away from the present. We either regret the things we did not do or feel ashamed about the things we did.

Similarly, thinking about the future can also distract us from the task at hand. Being overly excited about what will come next implies that what is in the present is lesser in value and not worth celebrating. This misconception that the past was better or the future would be more fabulous always keeps us chasing the perfect moment.

However, one should realise that no matter how far you chase the concept of perfection, it would never be within your reach if you follow this philosophy of looking for it in either direction. Instead, you should yearn for perfection in the present and concentrate on the task at hand. The here and now is the only place where you will create and celebrate something of value. It is only the present moment where you can be in sync with your mind and body. No mind is not an unnatural state; it is how the mind needs to be. The mind is most efficient, calm, and collected when conscious of the present moment.

> *"Paradise is within you, in your state of no-mind. And hell is also within you, in your very mind."*
>
> – Rajneesh

Many people cannot let go of their past; they feel guilty and keep going over possibilities, things that could have taken place if they had done something differently.

On the other hand, some people are so busy making plans for their future while ignoring all blissful moments in the present. They think that the events in the future will make them happy and fulfilled. However, this is far from the truth; real life happens in the present. The no-mind state allows you to only think about the present and not dwell over the past or get anxious about the future. Sure, learning from the past is essential, and planning is also an intelligent strategy; however, the problem arises when sacrificing our present to overthink these directions.

Involve in Everything but Entangle in Nothing

> *"Detachment does not mean non-involvement. You can be deeply involved but not entangled."*
>
> – Sadhguru

One cannot experience life without involvement, from the simplest and easiest tasks to the most sophisticated ones. Every activity and the day-to-day tasks require your involvement, so the goal should be to get involved in life rather than be entangled in it. Getting involved with people, knowing them, and learning about their lives isn't a dangerous thing to experience. On the contrary, it's the fundamental nature of a human being to seek company.

If you think that getting involved in a person's life means that their problems become your problems, then you are wrong. That's entanglement, not involvement.

There's no doubt that man is a social animal, and to live a blissful existence on this Earth, one must have a certain level of social involvement with others, especially with their kin such as family and siblings. There are also secondary sources of involvement, such as your friends and work. However, if you sit down and count your attachments to this world, you'll probably name those mentioned above as the most important. These social involvements are essential for everyone because you cannot spend your whole life alone. Therefore, it would be best to be involved with people to make connections and relationships.

However, most people go wrong with this; they involve themselves in certain relationships with specific roles. They form a bubble around themselves and think they can spend their lives hidden inside that bubble. This mistake of forming discriminatory involvements leads people to entanglements. The relationships you formed and the roles you fulfilled start looking like a job. The same bubble you once thought offered protection now feels like a prison cell, and your involvements start looking like shackles. Therefore, it is imperative to let your involvement be indiscriminate. Also, it is essential to understand that you are connected with everything; no bubble or cell can keep you from getting involved in the world's workings.

Your mere existence is an involvement in the matters of the cosmos, and your existence has had a presence, an effect on how situations have unrolled themselves. Therefore, instead of binding yourself to your involvements, let your involvements become indiscriminate. Realise that you are involved in everything that surrounds you; the Earth you walk upon, the food you eat, the water you drink, the air you breathe, and the very space in which you exist. Sounds too much, right? That is because not all these involvements are conscious; you are always unconsciously involved within your surroundings. For example, if you were not involved with the air that you breathe, you would suffocate. You just have to become conscious of the workings surrounding you, and you will understand that this is the way life is; it is full of involvements.

Think in Broader Terms

For a minute, stop your thoughts and think about the sun and moon, which follow a proper timetable. Think about the Earth, which spins, and the seasons that change at a particular time. How all the life on Earth is bound by the rules of nature. The flowers that bloom in a specific season, the birds that migrate in a particular season—everything around you is happening in sync. Yet, you feel awful, one nasty little thought is crawling through your mind, and you decide that the rest of your day will also be awful and full of terrible happenings. The problem is you have lost perspective of who you are. You have confined yourself to the measly attachments of the day-to-day rumblings of life. As a result, you have started to think too much of yourself.

You think your life experience is limited to who you are and how you are living. But take a step back and ask yourself, who are you in this cosmos? Do the seasons not affect you, and do you not dress yourself according to them? Do you not get affected by the rain, heat, and snow? You think your cosmos is your city, town, or apartment. You think that only you can control everything within the vicinity of your personal cosmos.

However, that is a foul perspective. By secluding yourself from the cosmos and the workings of the universe, you are merely fooling yourself. As in the cosmos, you are not even a speck of dust. Your physical existence in the universe is a miraculous feat. As a physical existence, you are nothing. If you understand this, you will look at everything in the world with absolute wonder and involvement. When you adopt this outlook and see from a broader perspective, you will understand that one little thought or emotion doesn't amount to anything. It's not something to be affected over and disrupt your mind.

> *"It's not what happens to you, but*
> *how you react to it that matters."*
> – Epictetus

You are the Cosmic Intelligence

Humans are created from the same matter that created the universe and its components. The matter of the universe, itself also created life and eventually, humans. Though, we are small and miniscule when compared to the grand scheme of things, our bonds with the universe are still strong. Although, most of us are unaware of these inseparable bonds, they exist, not as shackles that bound us to a certain extent but as cosmic ties that connect us to a larger stream of consciousness. These connections are ever expanding, and their benefits are countless only when we actively choose to pursue them. Consciously, we might fool ourselves with the notion of independency and loneliness; however, deep in our minds, our subconscious knows that these connections exist and cannot be severed. The matter of the universe tends to vibrate on a similar frequency as the matter that resides within us but the reason, we can't form a connection with it earlier in life is because our frequency is interrupted by the distractions and complications of worldly matters. Once we allow ourselves to focus solely on this endeavour to achieve the state of being cosmically intelligent, it's only a matter of patience and determination.

Experience the Moment

Experiencing the moment means simply being present in the moment happening right now. Your mind is designed to constantly fluctuate between a stressful thought about the future while simultaneously remembering a thought from the past, and you're stuck in the middle, not knowing what to do, how to feel or respond to the things happening with you in the present. It's the job of the mind to think and analyse everything. Whereas this is not a bad thing, it's certainly a chaotic situation to be in a state of constant thought and analysis. Such a state often leaves us confused about our actions in the moment. Therefore, there are a few ways you can calm and recalibrate your mind to the present.

> *"It's being here now that's important. There's no past and there's no future. Time is a very misleading thing. All there is ever, is the now. We can gain experience from the past, but we can't relive it; and we can hope for the future, but we don't know if there is one."*
>
> – George Harrison

The most effective activity to experience the moment is being in the 'no-mind' state; it allows you to stop thinking and focus on a single activity or exercise. It's not necessary that this activity must be something engaging like reading or painting. Concentrating on oneself during meditation also counts as an activity. The no-mind is like an off switch for your thoughts and distractions. To be present in the moment and concentrate on the task at hand, the no-mind state is a perfect state to be in. Whether it's the thoughts of worry, pain, or joy, the no-mind state blocks them all. When you are in this state, you will be thinking about is the here and now. You'll be conscious of your existence, and your mind will be empty.

Activities such as breathing techniques and meditation practices are some of the few best exercises that will help train your mind to be calm and present. Meditation, especially, allows you to listen to the beating of your own heart. It allows you to be in sync with yourself. It allows your mind to be in sync with the body. Breathing, on the other hand, allows you to control your pulse; it allows you to control the beating of your heart. It is a great way to relieve you from the anxieties and troubling thoughts of the future. Once you gain control over your body and bring it in sync with your mind, you will feel elevated, and your perception of your surroundings will become more transparent and wiser.

Once you are able to stop the disorganised thoughts in your mind, you will be able to communicate and act with confidence in the present. So often, we let our minds interfere with day-to-day actions, which has a significant effect on our lives and how we see the world. We let our past interfere with our present by judging a situation based on how it was instead of considering how it is. For example, you might feel discouraged and irritated if your friend doesn't accept your calls. Most of us, in such situations, refuse to give the benefit of the doubt to people and fall prey to our minds, which enforces the emotions of betrayal on us. We become biased because of our past experiences and tend to make the wrong decisions, which also has a significant effect on our future later in life.

The act of living in the moment can only be achieved if you efficiently stop all the chaotic thoughts popping up inside your head. All these thoughts tend to clutter your mind and distract you from the crucial issues. Take the example of an office worker who constantly daydreams about how his life will be when he gets a promotion, but what ends up happening is that because of his daydreaming, he ends up making a lot of mistakes and ends up submitting his work later than everybody else. Whether it's the anxiety of the future or the regret of the past, these factors affect an individual negatively and significantly impact his present situation.

It is imperative to live in the moment and fully experience the bliss and joy. This joy cannot be found in either of the other two directions of our life. Only the present holds the most opportunities and possibilities for us. Through living in the moment, you will be able to experience the joy of living. It'll help you understand why there is no time like the present. The wonders of the worlds, the life that is happening around you right now, is the most precious, and among all these miracles is you, a creature able to comprehend the beauty of the cosmos. You will be able to appreciate all that the universe has given you once you look at it from a recalibrated point of view. It is a point of view that neither holds any past bias against it nor complains about it being different than you imagined. You will see the world as it is, right now, in the moment.

CHAPTER 9
ACCESSING THE COSMOS

Significance of Meditation for Me

The practise of meditation has become fascinating nowadays. People from all walks of life are being attracted to this magic word. However, the agony is that this serene practise has become distorted in many ways.

In this day and age, many different variants of meditation exist—meditation with alcohol or drugs and several other types of guided meditations. Unfortunately, almost all are nothing more than cheap relaxing techniques.

These practises go entirely against the purpose of meditation. More than 99% of the people talking about it see it as a tool for mental peace or a method to reduce their daily stress. All of humanity has become so engrossed in this materialistic world that it is challenging for them to think beyond this body and mind.

The actual purpose of meditation is far more profound and divine than people usually think it to be. The purpose of meditation is to achieve self-realisation;

all other benefits are automatically achieved along the journey.

Unfortunately, we have deviated from our objective and entangled ourselves in the web of our desire. On the other hand, there's also no doubt that this misconception regarding meditation has resulted in more people getting themselves into it.

Even when I started meditating, I was merely looking for a way to destress my mind as I was under tremendous pressure from my employer and family. In addition, I was declared a pre-diabetic who was also on pills for high blood pressure. All these adversities forced me to find solace in the practise of meditation.

Since then, I have been regularly meditating. Initially, it was challenging to sit still, even for a couple of minutes. All sorts of negative thoughts used to surround me from all sides. These thoughts were so disturbing that they refused to let me sit quietly. As soon as I closed my eyes, scenes from the past flooded my mind one after another. The memories of my insult, hurt, pain, setbacks, failure were so powerful that I was utterly helpless in front of them. One thought triggered another; *I should have told this, I should have done that, I could have done better*, etc.

My mind was occupied with devising strategies for the events in my life that were already in the past. Despite being in my rear-view with no significance on my current situation, they constantly made rounds in my consciousness.

Later, I was taught the proper techniques to anchor my mind on something rather than letting the thoughts flow by my Guru. Gradually, I discovered ways to keep my mind focused on myself. Slowly, I saw the duration of my meditation increase.

After meditating intermittently for 4-5 months, I discovered that my usual high blood pressure had significantly decreased. That was the only reason I continued with my meditation. I found out that when I used to stop my practise for a month or so, my blood pressure shot up to a higher number.

As time passed, my negative reflections turned into neutral ones, and even though all old thoughts still invaded my mind now and then, the impact they had on me had reduced. I was not disturbed by these thoughts anymore.

Meditation

Yama and Niyama

There are a few things to take care of before diving into the practise of meditation. First, meditation will not start showing any impact unless your mind and body are not in the path of purity. Therefore, it is essential to follow some abstinence for purity. Understandably, it is challenging for some people to stay away from the habits they have been taught since childhood. But if you practise, you can make it possible and rid yourself of all the destructive patterns. There are five different branches of abstinence; in Sanskrit, they are called 'Yama':

- Non-violence – Try not to harm any living and non-living being.

- Stay truthful – Stay away from concealing anything. This gives us yet another layer of our identity.
- Refrain yourself from committing any acts of theft.
- Chastity – Sexual activity provides us maximum memory to our system. As we try to dissolve all our identities, this is not good for our spiritual practices.
- Non-possession – Any accumulation slows down the process of self-realisation. Be it physical, mental, or worldly objects, they all deviate us from our objective.

Once you start abiding by these rules, the next step is to teach the habit of being pure, called Niyama in Sanskrit. Niyama also involves several steps; some are as follows:

- Cleanliness: Cleanliness of body, mind, speech, and our environment
- Contentment and acceptance: Be content with whatever you have and accept the situation other people are facing. It is because of their unique situation they behave differently.
- Self–Discipline: There are various aspects of this habit. Putting honest effort into our goal, for example, practicing austerity and asceticism towards our practices.
- Self–Study: This is to enhance our knowledge about our real self. It is not only about studying

other books but reading your own thoughts, emotions, and actions in each moment.

- Contemplating the authentic self: Spend every moment by contemplating our own self, which is nothing but an unchanging reality.

Asana

Feeling relaxed and comfortable are a few fundamental requirements of meditating. Therefore, to feel comfortable and steady, you are required to perform asanas. This makes our body and mind focussed and intense. Asanas are nothing but various poses of Yoga. Asanas are also responsible for a balanced Nadi system in our body. Therefore, asanas directly affect our earth element and improve balance.

Pranayama

Pranayama works with Vayu (air) element. Vayu is the most significant element as we cannot sustain our lives without breathing for five minutes. Pranayama provides us with the ability to work with and control our Vayu element. In this stage, we consciously regulate our breath. This meditation dramatically enhances the focus of our minds.

Pratyahara

Pratyahara combines two words, Prati (against) + Ahar (fetch). It is a fact that sensory organs drive a human being and create desire and attachment with the external world. In this process, we consciously focus on not becoming indulged with our senses. This practise is not about restraining our feelings but not indulging in the pleasure of our senses. This exercise will train your mind not to be affected by emotions as quickly and always balance your emotional state. Emotions create the water element as it is the nature of the water element to keep flowing. Similarly, our feelings also keep changing continuously. When we learn to separate ourselves from our emotions, the stage of pratyahara is successfully achieved.

Dharna

Our mind is usually indulging in the thoughts of the past or the future. We hardly spend a moment of our life living in the present. In Dharna, we consciously shift our focus from the past and future to the present. When we have control over our thoughts, it is straightforward to focus as per our wishes, but the most critical point is to learn to hold that focus for a long time. Each one of us must have experienced the momentary focus while studying, listening to music, or while highly indulging ourselves in any activity. These moments are often short-lived. Therefore, in Pratyahara, we lay the preparations for Dharna. We try to focus our minds on a single point. The goal is to attain that stage when the mind can concentrate without distraction from the outside world, including your own emotions. This practice is related to the fire element. As we keep advancing in our spiritual journey, we balance every component of our existence.

Dhyana

Dhyana is achieved after a lot of practise of the earlier six stages. Slowly and steadily, we keep decreasing the thoughts in our mind and advance to delta brain waves, where there are hardly any thoughts left in our mind. This practise is related to the fifth element called Ether. This stage of meditation often starts with a fraction of seconds which grows into minutes and hours. Once we come out of this meditation, we have complete control over our thoughts. You'll be able to think as per your wish; if it's not your wish to think, then your mind will be empty.

Samadhi

It might be wrong to say that this is the ultimate state of our being. However, it is a state where the difference between you and other living organisms is reduced to almost nothing. This is the realisation of "Cosmic Intelligence." Not only by our intelligence but by our experience, we realise who we are. It is the first step of our spiritual advancement. But in case someone attains this state, one should be able to differentiate oneself from one's body, mind, and energy. This state allows you to unlock various dimensions of your existence.

My Experience with Meditation

In March 2020, we shifted to a new apartment; here, I prepared one room on the third floor to be my healing room. In this room, I used to practise my therapies such as hypnotherapy, sound therapy, and other forms of healing. I also kept this room energised with the help of crystals, flowers, flowing water, winds, and candles. Hence, keeping the environment conducive to therapy, healing, and meditation practises.

After every therapy session, I cleared out the energy emitted. These therapies are helpful to those who are suffering from any psychological and emotional issues. Here I got some quiet time for my meditation and yogic practises as well. This room was also secluded, and there was minimum interference from kids or any other visitors. Every now and then, I meditate for one and a half to two hours at midnight for minimal interference.

The Tap Water Dilemma

Let me share with you all a phenomenon that occurred to me. While meditating one day, I heard a sound; it sounded like someone had left the tap water flowing. After some time, the sound stopped, only to resume after a few seconds. This kept happening, and I was left wondering who could be playing with the tap water in the dead of night. The following day when I sat for meditation, I felt the same way. I was unsure if my kids were playing with the water tap or if someone in my neighbourhood was doing it. I became annoyed with this sound and felt I had made a mistake by renting this house.

This same phenomenon kept happening in the days to come. What surprised me the most was that someone decided to play with the tap water only when I sat down to meditate. I was so annoyed that one day I asked my sons why they played with the water tap at midnight. However, they were utterly clueless about what I said.

My sons and wife even started to joke that I had gone crazy because of my meditation. That is when I realised that this could be related to my meditation.

The next time I sat down to meditate, I was cautious and noticed that the sound was absent. I did not hear any water sound, and this peace continued for a few days. Then suddenly, this sound arrived again only to vanish as soon as I became cautious of it.

This whole affair continued for a few days until I realised that this was the sound of my own breath. My consciousness magnified the process of breathing in and breathing out. It sounded like tap water flowing. After a few minutes, when the mind and body calm down, breathing becomes deeper and deeper. With every inhalation, I experienced someone switching on the tap. With every exhalation, it sounded as if somebody was switching the tap off. After this realisation, the sound completely stopped and never came back.

Effect of the Full Moon

The day of the full moon is considered important for many reasons. Mainly because the cosmic pull between two heavenly bodies, the sun and moon, is quite strong on such a day, affecting even the ocean. The beings that live on the earth are also not untouched as they contain a very high percentage of water in their bodies.

Usually, on full moon day, I observe a fast. I refrain from eating anything the entire day, and in the evening, I worship the moon and break my fast. Initially, my fasting did not have anything to do with my meditation as there was a different reason for doing it. But when you are in meditation and raise your vibration to resonate with the cosmos, you can experience something unusual. So, on this full moon day, I learned the benefits of my fasting.

For the last few days, I felt interferences while meditating in the daytime. So, I decided to start meditating early in the morning. On that night, I slept at 10:30 pm and woke at 3:15 in the morning. The moonlight was illuminating my healing room. At 3:30 am, I sat down for meditation just below the window through which I could see the radiance of the moon in the clear night sky.

After the initial breathing exercises, I started meditating. I struggled for a few minutes to concentrate. But soon, my breathing was in a rhythm, and I understood that I was going deeper and deeper into meditation. After some time, I went into a deep trance.

Suddenly, a loud noise penetrated my head. It started with a low pitch but gradually reached its pinnacle, where the sound had become intolerable for me. It became hard to keep my eyes shut with the ear-piercing sound. I quickly opened my eyes and found that the whole world was still dark. There was complete silence in the outside world, and there was an effulgence of moonlight amid the darkroom.

I was not sure what happened to me or what that sound was. I didn't know if I was awake or asleep. Was it a dream, or was it real? I was completely perplexed. I kept myself in the same position, carefully perceiving each palpitation and feeling them all over my body. I could easily sense my body moving with each heartbeat. And after some time, I felt everything going back to normal. It was 4:47 am now; I got up and went back to sleep.

I woke at 8:25 am and was still thinking it was a dream. The memory of that experience was too strong for it to be a dream. Therefore, I concluded that this was the first knock of the consciousness on my Anahat (heart) Chakra. My consciousness crossed my Manipuraka (Solar Plexus) Chakra and hit Anahat Chakra.

The actual journey started from here.

The Anahat Naad

It was another full moon day as well as the beginning of a new month. On this day, I started two new practises. One practise would last for the next year, i.e., till 30th September 2021, while the other, I decided to continue for the rest of my life (unless it becomes impossible to perform).

On this day, I received great news from my wife. She was pregnant with our third baby. I was late to start my meditation on that day as I had to attend a medical appointment with her. By the time we came back home, it was already 9:45 am. I laid down in "Shavasan" for a while to relax my body and calm my mind. I got up and sat down to start meditation around 10:30 am. Usually, I set the alarm for two hours, but I did not set any alarm that day. I put my cell phone on mute and kept it nearby.

It was a cloudy day, and the temperature was close to 16 degrees Celsius in the morning. I sat down in "Dhyan Mudra" with my folded legs in "Sukhasan." I started with breathing exercises which included "⊠" breathing, chanting, Shwan breathing, and Bandhas. It took me almost 20 minutes to complete these breathing and chanting practises. Then, I took in a deep breath in and closed my eyes with an affirmation of going deeper into meditation. A wave of thoughts started arriving in my mind. One after the other, thoughts flooded my consciousness. They were related to every issue, all the known and unknown encounters, a scene from a recent Netflix series, job hunting, cooking food, childhood memories with my grandfather in the mango orchard, childhood dreams, and recent WhatsApp message from my favourite BHU group and whatnot.

Waves of thoughts kept hitting the shore of my mind one after another, and after every wave, I realised that they were all irrelevant. My main goal was to stop all thoughts so that my body was free from all emotions. I have been practising it for a while now. I could stop thoughts for some time between, and they emerged again from nowhere at the very next moment. This continued for a while as sometimes it takes a few minutes to reach a steady point where you can control your thoughts. I experienced some sensation in my prefrontal cortex while controlling those mental intrusions.

After trying several times, I was finally able to control my thoughts. I found myself in a stupor without any struggle once my thoughts were under my control, and it was not long before I started hearing soothing music.

I thought the kids must have started playing it because, usually, Khushi, my wife, listens to songs in the morning. I did not let my attention divert because of this music. However, soon I realised that the sound was increasing and with it my discomfort to it. This time I understood that it was happening within me. I heard a similar sound a few months ago, and I got scared.

This time I made up my mind to allow myself to get into it. Suddenly, I saw a flash of light, and the music was dialled up to the maximum volume. It was challenging to figure out any definite pattern of the notes. After a few seconds, I noticed the shape of a person with his hands resting on his folded legs. It looked exactly how I used to sit in meditation. I was not sure if it really was me or just a shadow of mine. The figure was completely dark, and a bright light was illuminating in the background.

To my dismay, I was struggling with this high-pitched sound and high-intensity light when I suddenly sensed myself getting lighter. My body started lifting. The lower part of the body barely touched the cushion I used to sit and meditate. My heart started pounding, and I checked if I was asleep. I could sense my head was tilted a bit and realised that all the sensations were real. As soon as I started gathering my consciousness, the feeling of weightlessness faded, the light and sound started disappearing.

Even though I wanted to continue being in this state, everything looked like a dream and vanished in no time. My arms were still so light, my mind was calm, and I could feel every particle of my body full of energy. After leaving this state, I continued to sit in the same position.

I was thinking about the experience repeatedly, trying to replay it in my mind. I wish I would not have checked my awareness. Those moments of tranquillity were priceless, and I wanted to experience more of them. I had an idea of what was happening to me at that time; someone had once explained it all to me; they told me that when consciousness reaches Anahat chakra, people start feeling lighter, hear sounds, and may even see a flash of light.

Beyond the Anahat

It was the fifth day of the auspicious time of Navratri. This is the time of high cosmic vibrations. During this period, there are numerous examples of people attaining their unfulfilled desires by simple tantric and yogic techniques. On this day, I started meditating at 9 am in my healing room; however, I was completely unaware of the experience I was about to have. Usually, I meditate for 1.5 to two hours and then do my Puja, Jap, and Paath. Usually, it takes almost three hours to complete my spiritual and religious practices every day.

After about one and a half hours, I was about to get up and start other practises, but I was still in deep meditation. Suddenly, I felt that I was in an ocean, floating in the water. A sense of fear crept up in my mind and gave me goosebumps all over my body; I got scared and felt as if I was going to drown. But at the same time, my mind reassured me, and I said to myself, "I can handle this situation. I am not going to drown for sure".

I started chanting Krishna's name repeatedly and asked Lord Vishnu to get me out of this glut of water.

I felt myself floating down and down, and after a few seconds, a buoyant force of water started propelling me towards the surface of the water. My whole body had a delightful sensation. Soothing music continuously played in my mind as I felt myself levitate off the water's surface and had goosebumps all over my body. To make sure that I was awake, conscious, and not dreaming, I pressed my upper teeth against the lower teeth and assured myself that I was not sleeping. The experience of weightlessness and levitation was very much real while I was still awake. The sensation of wafting up and down continued for a while.

Sometime later, it all stopped, and I started feeling my hands in the Dhyan Mudra, folded legs, straight neck and head. Finally, I emerged to my complete awareness. I kept sitting there for some time, smiling on my own, trying to replay the experiences I'd just had in my mind.

When the consciousness moves beyond Anahata Chakra and has not reached Vishudhdhi Chakra yet, the air element takes over. As the air element is prominent in the Anahata chakra, its activation usually feels lighter and lighter for people. In some cases, people also feel like levitating.

Fly High

It was the day of Kartik Poornima, one of the holiest full moon days in Hindu tradition. This day is celebrated differently in various parts of the world, and for us, it is "Kojagara Poornima." On this very auspicious day, people worship the Goddess of abundance to get all sorts of abundance in their lives. It is said that the cosmic vibration on this day is so high that with simple techniques and a little bit of practise you can fulfill your desires.

I had prepared myself for this day, as I had experienced the feelings of tranquillity on the last full moon while meditating. I made up my mind that I was going to spend these two days meditating without any distractions. I also selected my food carefully, as there are some food items that are not conducive to the meditating body and mind. Overeating can also destroy this opportunity to experience your body and mind in its true self. Therefore, on the 30th of October, 2020, I had a very light dinner and decided that I would get up after mid-night and meditate for the rest of the night. I had also decided to trust myself this time to not make the mistake of checking my awareness because doing so takes the individual out of the tranquil state.

Everything was going as per my plan except for the fact that I could not sleep, as it was Saturday on the 31st, the kids took some time to go to bed. Once they went to sleep and the world became serene and calm, I went upstairs to my healing room and sat down in "Sukhasan." It took almost 20 minutes to complete my initial breathing exercises and chanting before starting meditation. Slowly and gradually my body and mind were ready to go into deep meditation. Initially, I struggled with thoughts popping up from all directions, but after some time, my mind went into an endless void state.

After a while, the upper part of my body felt a sudden shake, and goosebumps spread from head to toe.

There were no visuals this time nor a high-pitched sound, but I could feel my body becoming weightless. A soothing sensation had spread all over my body. All I could hear was a humming sound, and I felt my body moving upwards. After some time, I came back to my awareness. It was a great experience. The next night there was a full moon, and I was very excited, but it was 3:45 am, and it was important for me to sleep well as meditation would work better only then.

The next morning, I got up around 7:30 am and started meditating after my usual morning chores. I hoped to experience more wonderful and otherworldly experiences. My mind and body came into sync after a while, and I could feel my breath going into a rhythm. I kept sitting for some time and my mind was getting deeper and deeper into meditation. However, two hours passed, and I realized that I should get up as there was no experience this time. I decided to preserve my hope for the evening and night.

I had a very light breakfast and skipped my lunch that day. In the evening after pooja, I started meditating again. It was 7:30 pm on my watch when I decided to meditate. I sat for almost an hour and a half when my son came upstairs to ask me to come down for dinner. I was disappointed as I was not able to have a similar profound experience as the one I'd had the day before, but I decided not to give up and keep trying to meditate as I had been doing for the last few years.

Circular Geometrical Object

For the past couple of days, when I wake up in the night, I feel as if something is revolving in both my eyes. This is that circular geometrical structure, nicely drawn in black and white. Ever since we shifted to Perth, it had become difficult to sit for a long time and meditate. But I make sure to continue the practise of meditation at least 2-3 times a week. On this day, I woke up around 4:50 am, and after finishing my morning chores, I sat down to

meditate. During the initial practise of stopping my thoughts, I realised that doing so has become easier. I can stop my thoughts for short durations without much struggle. Soon I was into a deep trance. After some time, I started hearing the same humming sound and was able to see that revolving circular geometrical object revolving above my head. Everything was happening very quickly, I wanted to stay in the same state but soon everything dissolved and vanished completely. I knew I had to free myself from the burdens of my new job and the new city to experience it for a longer time.

The Blue Sun

It was a new moon last night. The moon was setting in the Pisces. Saturn, Jupiter, and Mars were visible in the sky. This was a specific day when intuition is intensified. I did not know about this combination. As usual, I woke up at 4 am, and after finishing my morning chores, I sat down in meditation. It was Sunday, and I did not need to go into work, so I did not set the alarm on my phone. Otherwise, I have a habit of setting an alarm for one and a half hour and then start meditating.

The last 3-4 months were too hectic for me as I had recently shifted to Perth from Sydney. Apart from a couple of occasions, I could not experience anything during meditation due to this shift in the environment. I started to meditate at 4:37 am, and it was easier now to empty my mind of all thoughts and collect my consciousness entirely as I did not have to wait for long to get into a deep trance.

After some time, I had the same feeling of going upwards, so I let myself lose and flew even higher. As I was going upwards, the circular geometrical object from the last time appeared again. It was revolving right in front of me; however, this time, it was not just a shape, it had a color and light too.

A dazzling light filled my entire view. Something as powerful as the sun was shining over my head. Initially, I was not able to see anything, but slowly when I tried to observe carefully, I was able to see it as a blue colour with a yellowish patch on it. Suddenly, I felt as if my throat was parched. I thought it must be my illusion, and tried to get over this feeling. I also felt that I was not able to move my lower jaw. For some time, it felt like I would die due to the choking and dry throat. I tried to at least swallow the saliva in my mouth, but I was not able to do that. As I was trying hard the thing revolving over my head started making a sound. It was a very uncomfortable situation. I once again tried to swallow some saliva in my mouth, but my jaw was not letting me do that. I had never faced this kind of situation in the past. As I was trying hard to get over this, I moved my consciousness. Slowly the revolving object slowed down and vanished. I was still flying. When I finally came back to my senses, my throat was really dry, and I wanted to drink lots of water. Though I did not find anything unusual with my jaw, it was perfectly fine. I rubbed my palm and got over this trance state.

This was another milestone in my journey. The colour of the throat chakra is blue, and I think the blue colour signified that the consciousness had risen to the Vishudhi Chakra. Though few moments during the trance were terrifying, when I think about it now, I feel really good.

While meditating, I have experienced weightlessness a few times. As I started feeling weightless, I became alert, and the experience of being light and weightless vanished at once. On few occasions I also experienced, as if I am rising and moving clockwise at the same time. I realised that as long as I focus on staying alert, my journey will not progress because when we are alert, our mind prompts that something is happening to us. The sense of being us or the feeling of being 'me' destroys all the experiences. As our consciousness progresses higher, it reminds us that we are different from the mental and physical. Any alertness makes us limited to this mind and body. I am still waiting for the day when I shall be free from the senses of my own identity; and therefore, my journey continues.

CHAPTER 10

PRACTISE AND EXERCISE TO ACTIVATE THE COSMIC INTELLIGENCE

Now that we have arrived at the final phase of this book, let us go back to the roots, the fundamentals on which this book basis itself on—cosmic energy.

> *"Opening your chakras and allowing cosmic energies to flow through your body will ultimately refresh your spirit and empower your life."*
>
> – Barbara Marciniak

Cosmic energy is the driving force of life which exists all around us. The cosmos, the molecules, the space between galaxies and space itself is filled with cosmic energy. It is a vital force that maintains order in life and assists humans in expanding their consciousness. Only the beings who can be at peace with themselves and can live in the present moment can become receivers of cosmic energy. Achieving cosmic energy provides a being with countless benefits, but the main characteristic of a cosmically intelligent being is "Blissfulness," a state of mind formed after combining peace, love, and joy.

Many of you might know this concept as trusting your gut, listening to your "instincts," tapping into your Higher Self, tuning into your sixth sense or plugging into cosmic intelligence—all these describe the same kind of experience and refer to cosmic energy. This ability allows you to acquire knowledge without conscious thought. Simply put, the ability to bypass the usual linear nature of thought and directly perceive or comprehend a truth is a characteristic related to a higher cosmic intelligence. A higher cosmic intelligence allows a person to skip the lengthy mental process and jump straight to the conclusion. Take an example of a person who is good at catching a lie or learns quickly. These types of quirks directly relate to having high cosmic intelligence. The power to perceive the truth, to see behind walls and realise facts, has been ability that is inside every human being since birth. It is an inherent guidance system built within us to keep us safe from harm and lead us to the best of circumstances that will assist the growth and evolution of our consciousness.

But how does it work? Well, for many people it is hard to understand these concepts because people have become too shallow and self-obsessed. They fail to see anything that is beyond themselves and their problems. These people are merely blinded by the fogs of doubt and selfishness, and thus, their minds have become shallow. They think, "How could I, a tiny human being in this whole wide world, in an infinitely vast universe, have direct access to something like cosmic intelligence?" The doubts of these people are justified; after all, how a person can make any sense out of an invisible, non-material mechanism that is impossible to be realised by their own five senses. The answer to their question can be found in a philosophical model of reality known as the *holographic universe.*

You might be familiar with the idea and concept of holograms. A hologram is a three-dimensional image constructed with the help of a laser light. The interesting thing about this is, in the production of the hologram, the full image is contained in even the smallest fragment of the original photographic plate. This is why it is named hologram, as 'holo' means whole or complete and gram refers to the smallest piece. Coming over to the connection this has with cosmic intelligence in the teachings of Vedanta, specifically the Atharva Veda, you find the metaphor of *Indra's Net.* The metaphor of Indra's Net compares the world to a net woven by the great deity Indra. This net is said to be infinite and spread in all directions with no beginning or end and at each junction point in the net is a jewel that reflects all other jewels. No jewel exists separately from the rest; all jewels are connected and interdependent—every being contains the entire universe within itself. This overwhelming understanding is encapsulated in two Sanskrit sutras:

- *Aham Brahmasmi:* I am the Universe.
- *Tat Tvam Asi:* I am That.

This theory states that you, a being, are a node in the system of the universal network and connected with everything that exists, has existed, or will exist. Your cosmic mind is directly plugged into the cosmic mind of the universe. The cosmic mind knows the answer to every question and the truth behind every event. The cosmos is the absolute authority and you, by definition, have access to the field of cosmic intelligence. You are merely too distracted by mental, physical and emotional circumstances of your life and too consumed by the worldly interferences to realise and comprehend your cosmic intelligence.

Overall, cosmic energy is the foundation of all our actions, reactions to situations and circumstances that take place in and around us. When we are in a state of rest or sleep, our body receives cosmic energy due to the peaceful and silent state. If we look at cosmic energy as per Hindu philosophy, it is known as Prana. In Hindu philosophy, cosmic energy is thought to be the source of '*kundalini.*' Many new age authors refer to this energy as quantum zero vacuum point energy and as orgone energy. Following are the reasons why cosmic energy is essential:

- To maintain an orderly life
- To lead a happy and healthy life
- To obtain knowledge
- To be completely involved in all the situations in life
- To expand our consciousness

Our body and mind are always surrounded by an energy field; this field is nourished by cosmic energy and helps in the healing of our physical, mental, and spiritual self. Cosmic energy is positive in nature and reduces negativity; it also aids in complete healing and creates a sense of harmony and balance in life. Some physical benefits of cosmic energy are listed below:

- Cosmic energy regulates blood flow and lowers stress on the heart.
- Cosmic energy helps in lowering cortisol and lactate levels in the body. These chemicals are often associated with mental stress and illnesses.
- Cosmic energy helps in eliminating free radicals from the body.
- Cosmic energy does wonders in treating all types of psychological issues such as anxiety, irritability, and depression.
- Cosmic energy also aids in healing cardiovascular diseases and promotes the development of skin resistance.
- Cosmic energy helps improve memory function and plays an excellent role in enhancing the psychological self by supporting emotions and rejuvenating feelings.

Accessing Cosmic Intelligence

Now that you have understood what cosmic intelligence is and where it comes from, the question that must be arising in your mind now is that how you can tap into this state of higher intelligence. There are a few steps you should consider to expand your powers.

1. Understand Your Eternal Self

This is a vital step in the process of better understanding of your true self and the growth of your consciousness. The foremost step necessary for you to depart to a more beautiful state is to separate from the belief that you are an isolated being in the universe. As long as you believe yourself to be an ordinary speck, a tiny flesh-encapsulated being that is cut off from the rest of the world in a random and unintelligent universe, you will be subconsciously blocking the signals from the cosmos. Therefore, to begin properly you must realise your identity as a unique and powerful being in a web of universal consciousness.

2. Build the Intention to Receive Guidance

Form a crystal-clear intention to receive guidance. If your intentions are weak and faulty, there is no point in seeking guidance from anything or anyone. Set goals about what you want to achieve from your meditation and practises; you can also write your goals on a piece of paper so that your subconscious mind has more visual cues. You can also use positive and direct affirmations to reprogram your subconscious such as vocal chants.

3. Still Your Mind

To make your plane fly, it is imperative to clear the runway. A turbulent and chaotic mind will never be able to perceive cosmic guidance. If you try to pick up signals with a mind overwhelmed with thoughts and worries, it'll be impossible to comprehend any kind of cosmic knowledge. The output would be like listening to music on a static-filled radio station; you only get bits and pieces of the song. To practise a still mind, you can pick up several habits such as painting, listening to music, and writing or simply practise mindfulness.

4. Ask Questions

When your mind is still, inquire yourself and find out what worries you the most. Ask yourself and develop a strategy that helps you seek your insight. Your worry could be as little as a minor personal problem or as great as a major family issue. After pondering your problem for a while, know that the message has gone into the universal cosmic database for resolution and keep an open mind to seek answers.

5. Reach Out

After releasing your question into the cosmic database, try to visualise your awareness expanding into the world, enveloping your home, city, state, country, planet, galaxy, and far beyond. Feel your awareness encompass the entire universe.

6. Tune into Emotional and Physical State

Connect with your emotional and physical state, feel the world around you, and imagine your five senses activating one by one, noticing the sounds, sights, scents, and sensations of all kinds. Similarly, try to fathom the presence of others, their emotions, thoughts, and energy.

Train yourself to control your emotions to build and improve your senses. The more sensitive you become, the more easily you will be able to register the messages from the universe into your consciousness.

7. Trust the Message

After you heighten your senses, it will be easier for you to comprehend the subtle cues around you communicated by the universe. For example, when you notice an unfamiliar sensation in your body, a twinge, slight warmth in your stomach or chest, or the faintest level of feeling, tune into that and try to deconstruct it. Does the sensation feel good, or does it feel slightly uncomfortable? If you realise a good feeling, proceed towards that direction; on the other hand, if it feels uncomfortable or simply not good, pull back. Trust the subtle signs and follow them through. Similarly, if you receive an insight into an issue or problem you've been struggling with, trust the guidance. Once you completely comprehend that you're plugged into the cosmic mind and that it has an unusual way of doing things that often lack logical reasons, you'll find yourself in synch with every creation.

Practising all these steps will allow you to feel safe with the knowledge you're tapping into. However, this doesn't mean avoiding common senses or rational thinking. Remember cosmic knowledge is only a supplementary to the human mind. There's no doubt that the cosmos pulls information from a source far greater than a rational mind can fathom. The rational mind will naturally find intuitive guidance strange due to its limitations.

Regularly practise these steps to refine your mind as like any skill. Cosmic intelligence takes time to develop and master; however, if you are determined and consistent, a small spark will surely grow into a bright flame of wisdom and insight.

Cosmic Energy and Meditation

> *"Mediation is not spacing out or running away. In fact, it is being totally honest with ourselves"*
>
> – Kathleen McDonald

There is no end to the cosmic energy in the cosmos. This energy can be channelled using chakras, breathing exercises, and energy healing. However, the best and simplest way to acquire this positive energy is still through one of the original practices—meditation.

Modern science estimates that about 95% of our behaviour is run on autopilot. That's because our body is a complicated web of millions of neural networks, and processing all of these networks takes up too much time and energy. Therefore, our body reduces the millions of sensory inputs per second into manageable shortcuts so that fewer resources are spent in working out daily behaviours. Meditation is the exact opposite of this automatic state and default processes. Meditation allows us to take control our body's processes and enables us to carry out actions intentionally and consciously through willpower and decisions. Besides the fact that meditation is one of the best practices to become aware and fully comprehend the meaning of life, let's look at how it helps in receiving cosmic energy.

- The entry point for cosmic energy is our mind, and meditation directly impacts the mind and helps our mind to become focused and calm to better equip it to receive cosmic energy. Many experts suggest that cosmic energy is channelised through meditation. This meditation imparts calmness of mind and develops inner peace. When the mind is calm, it can receive cosmic energy more efficiently.
- Chakras, an essential part of achieving cosmic intelligence, are blocked in most individuals. This happens mostly due to mental and emotional distractions such as stress, anxiety, fear, and other negative emotions. Meditation allows cosmic energy to enter our system through the chakras and supports the independent energy field of the body.
- Meditation allows the mind and body to become one, thus making the physical and spiritual selves ready to receive cosmic energy.
- In the state of meditation, we often also focus on our breathing which allows us to absorb energy from our base chakra from the Earth. This way, one can increase the body's energy in a short time.

Overall, it is not wrong to state that cosmic energy can be felt and received effectively through a regular practise of meditation.

Synching Your Body's Geometry

You must have experienced this phenomenon yourself many times when you visit someone's house or a building and feel-good while being in that architectural space. This feeling of comfort and peace is not coincidental; in fact, there is a science to it. Sometimes when we look at people, things, or buildings and feel like looking at them for longer periods, it's due to their symmetry or geometric dimensions. Sure, you can say that beauty plays a role; however, that's not always the case. Even when the object that we are drawn to is not beautiful, we still want to keep looking at it. The main reason for that is that symmetry is intrinsic to all of life. Beauty is subjective, what one individual considers attractive might not be as attractive to the other; however, the perception of symmetry is universal, one must be a little sensitive and perceptive to recognise it.

Nature is filled with symmetry, whether you look at the way a tree expands its branches and takes its final shape to flower petals, patterns of a snowflake and blades of grass; everything from an atom to the cosmos promotes symmetry and everything can function in absolute order because of this very phenomenon. Even the tiniest misalignment can lead to a halt in existence. Thus, for anything to function at its best, it should be geometrically well-structured. The same is true for our body and that is where (Yoga) meditation comes in. The whole yoga system was

developed to align our body's physical geometry with the cosmic geometry. Out of all geometric shapes, an equilateral triangle is symmetrical, and if you remember, we discussed that chakras are also in the shape of a triangle.

When we talk about the composition of the human energy system, there are two equilateral triangles—one that points upwards and the other that points downwards. These two triangles meet just above the Anahata (heart chakra). The ideal alignment of these triangles would be a shape of perfect symmetry, at their absolute positions, these triangles intersect to form a perfect six-pointed star, forming six equilateral triangles at each extension. When this happens, it means that the system is in complete balance. Feelings of stress and anxiety are indicators that something has gone off in symmetry, causing friction in the system. Therefore, everything in the system must be well aligned.

Hatha yoga is one of the many yogic methods of aligning the inner system and adjusting to the geometry of the cosmos, this adjustment allows a person to become in sync with existence and achieve a balanced chemistry of health, joy, and balance. *Surya Namaskar* is another such process where you align yourself with the cycle of the Sun.

The 12 different mudras in Surya Namaskar, if repeated 12 times a day, align your life pattern with that of the Sun. In this matter, women are given an advantage as they have the natural privilege to follow the cycle of the moon due to their added responsibility of propagating the human race. It is essential to have balance between the sun and the moon for every human being, with hand mudras such as Chandra Mudra to balance the moon, and Surya Mudra to balance the sun. Other yoga poses which promote balance are: the tree pose[6], Cat pose, and Rocking Baby pose; all these meditation poses are helpful in balancing our geometry with that of the cosmos.

Synching with the Cosmic Vibrations

Yoga and other spiritual meditations are said to have one universal cosmic intelligent vibration. Often this vibration is articulated through the primitive sound of the combination of three letters such as AAAAAAAAAA...[7] OOOOOOOOOOOO... and MMMMMMMMMMMM... when combined it becomes AUM or OMM[8]. When chanted 21 times per day, this mantra helps in synching our Solar Plexus (Manipura Chakra), Heart Chakra (Anahat Chakra), and Throat Chakra (Vishudhi Chakra) with the cosmic energy. Other chanting mantras have different vibrations and because the cosmic vibration can be accessed by chanting the mantra OM repetitively, people who meditate regularly always seal their yoga practise by chanting this eternal sound vibration. Japa Mantra is another form of sound that allows an individual to tap into cosmic vibrations.

---

6 www.myeternalself.com/yoga

7 Refer to www.myeternalself.com/yoga for more detail

8 www.myeternalself.com/meditation

The chant Om is often called *pranava*, the sacred syllable, since it symbolises Cosmic Intelligence and the essence of spiritual reality. The mantra is said to connect individuals to others by acknowledging that we are all human and possess the same internal seeds of goodness and purity of heart. Chanting Om helps soothe the chaotic mind that can bring on negative feelings, such as anxiety and stress. It also helps purify the mind and allows us to move beyond the ego-based self to align with the Divine.

These cosmic vibrations have a huge positive effect on the body and can be used to heal the mind and the spirit as when you tap into this infinite spark of creativity, you can experience infinite healing on all levels. Therefore, chanting this mantra whenever you are feeling worried or stressed, simply chant OM for five to ten minutes and feel the cosmic vibration travelling throughout your body, envision the divine and healing you on every level of consciousness.

Synching with the Cosmic Energy

Earlier in the chapter of Chakras, we also discussed the Nadi system, which is equally important for our body as it is the system through which our energy flows. Our Nadi system is directly connected with the cosmos, but we don't experience it. If activated, it helps in activating our Chakra system (114 Chakras) and to activate these Nadis, there are practises that utilise the concepts of sun and moon energies. For example, Pranayama practices such as Nadi Shodhana also called channel cleansing breath or Alternate Nostril Breath, specifically target the Nadis[9]. Through these techniques, we isolate the Ida and Pingla Nadis by alternating which nostril we breathe through to create a balance between them.

The Nadis can also be activated by working with chakras. By awakening and activating specific chakras, we inevitably also awaken and activate the Nadis that intersect at that energy centre. Furthermore, Ida and Pingala Nadi are also associated with our sympathetic and parasympathetic nervous systems—you might have heard of the fight-or-flight and rest-and-digest responses. When we are more active, for example, when exercising, our fight-or-flight response kicks in, and Pingala Nadi is activated. On the other hand, when we are more relaxed, for example, restorative yoga our rest-and-digest response turns on, and we stimulate the Ida.

Ultimately, all yoga practises that fall under the huge umbrella of Hatha Yoga have the same goal in mind: to allow you to access the cosmos. Breathing techniques such as inverted U breathing (Anulom-Vilom), quick breathing (Kapalbhati), Bandhas[10]—Locking throat, Locking diaphragm and Locking root (Anus) are also a few techniques that stimulate your Nadi system.

The practise of meditation is undoubtedly a practise that can manifest wonders. I've said it before that it's not necessary to sit in a garden or under a tree to meditate, rather it's about your own dedication and intentions. By following the above-mentioned dos and don'ts, you will

9 Refer to www.myeternalself.com/pranayama

10 Refer to www.myeternalself.com/yoga

be able to dive into the ultimate experience of meditation and achieve the highest state of blissfulness.

Cosmic Intelligence is a state that every human being on this planet should strive to achieve as it allows a person to realise their real potential and deal with life more actively and intentionally. In a world where most people strive to live a blissful life, it's important to gain control of your life and live a fulfilled life and witness wholly the beautiful experiences cosmic intelligence and a blissful life offer.

MY NEXT RELEASES

Cosmic Intelligence – Sync in with the perpetuation

People are struggling with their own emotions such as sadness, anger, fear, surprise, disgust, love, care, joy etc. They all manifest on physical body in the form of distortion in thoughts, disease and depression. This book would shed light on the subtle part of our existence which is untouched from such emotional imbalance, once identified we are free from such emotional crisis. Few of the methods to get it identified are as under:

The moment experienced without any thoughts and emotions has the potential to create the whole universe. One such moment we experience so many times in a day. The moment between breath-in and breath-out. Be aware of these moments and they will extend to show you many lifetimes in that moment. A great process to be spiritually realized.

The whole universe moves in the cyclic order. Creation and destruction are the nature of the universe. We are simply unaware of similar ascendance and descendance in our breathing process. Breathing-in saves life, while breathing-out destroys the life. When there is no breathing-in after a breath-out, life ends. Be aware of that small curve where our breath changes the direction and the whole universe can be experienced. Transformation begins once such ascendance and descendance is observed so closely.

Don't identify any object with their attribute such as color, feel, sound, smell or taste. Just see the object as it is and you will dissolve in the beauty of the creation. There won't be any difference between you and the object. A practical process to end any relationship issues.

Don't get moved by your thoughts and no emotion would rise. Observe it from a little distance and all life-problems start vanishing slowly and slowly.

नवजात भिक्षुक

इस पुस्तक के हैं पात्र जिन्हें,
घर में रहना अधिकार नहीं ,
फुटपाथ, सड़क, नालों से बढ़कर,
स्वप्न कोई स्वीकार नहीं ।

यह नग्न सत्य कल्पना नहीं,
है प्रति पल की अनुभूति शेष,
हर पात्र याद कर सहमा हूँ,
निर्बल, निष्फल, अविरल अशेष ।

भले प्रगति को लेकर जितनी
आत्मप्रशंसा कर लें हम,
और भले मुख मोड़ सत्य से
आत्म वंचना कर ले हम ।

किन्तु शाप संताप मिटेगा,
इस जन जीवन से उस दिन,
हर शिशु को त्राण मिलेगा
और मान प्राप्त होगा जिस दिन ।

व्यथा हृदय के अतल व्योम में,
शब्द और सीमा से हीन,
मर्म विदारक अनुभव मन में,
घुले सदा अभिव्यक्ति विहीन ।

काश की यह कृति किसी,
एक नव भिक्षुक को नव जीवन दे,
कोई पुण्यमय, कोई दयामय,
उन्हें सदय संजीवन दे ।

CPSIA information can be obtained
at www.ICGtesting.com
Printed in the USA
LVHW092135040322
712645LV00002B/92

9 781637 677353